He Stilled the Storm Within Me

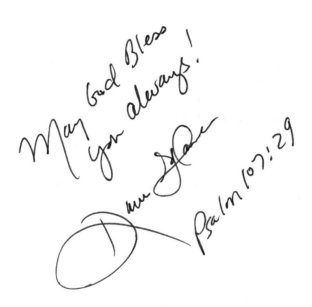

May God Bless you always!

Dawn Glaser

Psalm 107:29

Dawn Glaser

Dedication:

In loving memory of my grandmothers:

Nanny Powell, Granny King

and Mama Sandefur

Also, in honor of my mother:

Brenda Carroll Coyle

Praise God for the foundation each of these strong women laid down for my family!

Foreword

Dawn pours out her life as a love offering to her Savior in this courageous book. She is fearless in sharing her poignant story of pain and completing it with the victory of redemption in her life through our Lord Jesus Christ. She is transparent, vulnerable and authentic. May you be empathetic to her pain and filled with hope for your own future as you see her ability to overcome the obstacles in her path and move forward living a life purpose and fulfilling the destiny God created just for her.

Lori Kennedy,
founder of Alpha Omega Ministries, LLC

Acknowledgement

This book is a composite of my life in hopes that it will help others find their way out of the pit that I was so deeply in. I hope that they can find peace and salvation through Jesus Christ our Lord and Savior. I owe everything I have to God and am grateful for all He has done for me. I give Him the Glory for all that He has planned to do with this book. It is all for Him!

I would like to thank my husband, Chris, for his continued support through the years. He is my sweetheart for life and I am so grateful we never gave up on each other! I am thankful for my two boys, who continuously encourage and inspire me to be the kind of mother that God has planned for me to be. I would like to thank my mom who is always just a phone call away twenty-four hours a day, seven days a week. You are my sunshine when the clouds are gray and I love you dearly. I am grateful to God who places godly friends in my life in order to shape and mold me into the woman God intended me to be. You know who you are! I thank my sister for leading me to Christ as a teenager and my oldest sister for being there when our mom couldn't be when I was little. I thank my father and stepfather for their love and support over the years.

I am thankful for my church family, friends, and women's ministry bible studies. I would also like to thank Pastor David Roper for his outstanding preaching in order for a wretched soul like me to hear the call of Jesus and rededicate my life to Christ. I am thankful for my current Pastor Johnny Hunt whose preaching knows how to stir up the Holy Spirit in anyone who has ears to hear on any given Sunday. All of you have showed me how to step out of my comfort zone and live for Jesus through leadership, love, and loyalty! I would encourage any woman who has not taken a bible study to do so and be refreshed spiritually.

I am also grateful for God placing Dr. Susan Tanner, M.D. in my pathway. I owe her a huge thank you as well! To be medication free after so many years of bondage is a miracle in itself. Thanks for getting me back on track and for helping me claim the life I have always longed for. I am now ready to fight for what I believe in, take hold of my life again, and stand on my own two feet. I am physically and spiritually free!

I want to thank my editor, Stacy Yawn, and publisher, Nadine Yawn. Without the two of you, this book would not be possible. Your work is truly a labor of love, and I admire you with great respect. Thank you Amy Geist for your amazing photography and gift of creativity! God has given you a gift and I am grateful to call you my sister in Christ! Most of all I thank God for giving me this vision and never letting go of me! I cling to several bible verses that have helped me through the storms. However, Job 33:28 is my life verse! Thank you Father for redeeming my soul out of the pit so that I may live to enjoy the light!

Introduction

A lot of people may not want to give their entire testimony in a book or even tell it, for that matter. They may feel if they did they would give Satan all the fame instead of God, who brought them out of that despair. However, what about all of the ones who are going through what you have already been through? I believe people connect with others in knowing that they've been there. I feel like God allows us to go through crisis in our lives in order to help pull other people out of a similar situation they are going through. If I can help just one person by telling my entire testimony and prevent them from going down into the pit of depression, destruction, despair, and disillusionment, as I did, then it will all be worth it. I wish more women would be like the woman in the Bible who knew if she could just touch the garment of Jesus as he walked by, she would be healed. I also wish more women would open up about their lives and what they've been through like the woman at the well in Samaria in the Bible. She had a radical encounter with Jesus and let the whole town know about it in hopes that they would believe in Him also. I have skeletons in my closet that should probably stay there according to Satan, but, if I open the door to let others know how Jesus redeemed me, I won't regret it.

When I was twenty-two years old, a doctor diagnosed me with a mental illness, called "Bipolar Disorder". Most people know it as manic-depressive illness. I have to wonder what happened to trigger everything in my brain to go haywire. Why did it happen? Was it a misdiagnosis? Was it hereditary? Was it spiritual warfare? I had never heard of Bipolar Disorder before. When I was a teenager, I noticed I had a hard time comprehending things and remembering my notes in studying for exams. I could never remember things I read, or tell you about a movie I just watched a week before. These could possibly have been hints leading to my diagnosis. In my case, even though I was labeled with the diagnosis, I always felt that I caused it to happen. I never felt that it was something that I was born with and would have to accept. It ate at me constantly, and I couldn't shake the feeling that the finding was wrong.

I experienced a date rape at age sixteen and the doctors that I had seen in the past all agreed that because it was such a traumatic experience, it started the onset of Bipolar Disorder. I honestly think that the diagnosis is two-sided. The traumatic experience of rape caused such an emotional shock to me and blindsided me that my brain couldn't handle the emotions that came with it. I didn't find that out until twenty years later when I threw alcohol into the picture, causing the neurotransmitters in my brain to malfunction. Satan held me captive with emotional depression, anxiety, and fear for years. He had chains on me that were so tight, I felt as though the grip would last forever.

It took me twenty years to find the right doctor to agree with me and treat me. I hope if you are reading this and have ever been in bondage with Bipolar Disorder, fear, and depression or know a loved one that has, you will find the answers you need to heal and it won't take you as long as it took me. I was a daughter destroyed until God reminded me that I am a daughter of the King. My Pastor told us in church one Sunday that in the Bible, one of the greatest missionaries was Paul. Everywhere he went he told his testimony in hopes of bringing others to Jesus. Here is mine of how God brought me out of bondage.

Chapter One

Chaotic Cloudburst

When people hear the word "Bipolar Disorder", they run in the other direction. I had never heard that word until I was twenty-two years old and found myself in the mental ward of a local hospital in North Georgia. I'm not sure why this happened to me, but I can tell you that it took me twenty long years to get out of it and the bondage that came with the diagnosis.

It was a Friday night in the middle of the summer in Panama City, Florida. I had gone on a weekend retreat with some girls from work. I had a good job with a doctor in South Georgia and things between my husband, Michael, and I seemed to be going great until that weekend. The girls and I decided to go out to a local club for the night. We had been there for several hours and a guy came over and offered to buy me a shot. I accepted. The next thing I knew my mind seemed to be racing. I couldn't keep up with the conversations of the people around me. I felt dizzy and lightheaded. The guy that bought me the drink asked me to dance. I accepted that offer as well. The music was so loud. It was noisy, crowded, and very dark. People filled the room and I couldn't concentrate.

The guy I was with asked if I would like to go outside and get some fresh air. He reached down and kissed me, and before I knew it we were making out on a catamaran. I had my senses about me enough to remove myself from the situation and head back to my condo. By the time I got back everyone was asleep and it was morning. I hadn't had any sleep. My mind was still racing, and I could not focus. I felt so tired and knew I had a long drive back home. The guilt of not being a faithful wife was tremendous. One of the girls that I was with drove the entire three-hour trip back home. I had tried to sleep but all I could do was lie back on the head rest. When we got home, I got out of the car; next thing I knew, the very next day I started packing my car to leave my husband. I felt like the woman in the book of John, Chapter 8, who should have been stoned. The Pharisees wanted to condemn her for her adultery. Jesus told them, "Whoever is without sin, cast the first stone." Everyone left until no one was there but the woman and Jesus. No one was there to condemn her and Jesus told her to go and leave her life of sin. He forgave her. If only I had known. Like her, I was frightened and scared to death. I had no idea that I could have been forgiven. I ran instead. Michael was away at work and had no idea. I remember calling my girlfriend in Alsip, Georgia and asking her if I could stay for a while. She said that I could. We had known each other since we were in high school and still kept in touch. When I arrived at her house, I was talking very fast and could not eat anything.

It was the weekend, and we decided to go out to a night club in Atlanta. I started drinking again and the racing thoughts in my head were now so fast I that I became very frightened. I wasn't eating, sleeping, or thinking clearly. My girlfriend, Millie, asked me if I was doing drugs. I said, "No way." However, everything pointed in that direction. She searched my purse for drugs. There weren't any to be found. She called my dad because he lived nearby, and they both decided they should take me to the hospital. That's when a five minute consultation with a doctor started the beginning of a diagnosis that would label me forever.

I was asked to sign on the dotted line and, just like that, I was admitted to the mental ward of the top floor. They tried to give me medication. I refused. For the first three to four weeks I was completely out of mind. I was losing weight. I was not eating. My thoughts were horrific, and I was hearing voices. I heard a voice that told me to jump out the window to escape. I was singing a song called, "Morning has Broken" by Cat Stevens to the top of my lungs. Then the next day I heard a voice telling me to sing "Amazing Grace", by John Newton.

My husband, Michael, came to visit me with his sister. I had stuffed animals sitting around the table, and I was talking to them and setting their plate for tea time. You could tell by the look on my husband and sister in law's face, that something major was wrong with me. I tried to play the piano and sing out loud. I was totally out of my ever-loving mind!

The nurses couldn't handle me. They put me in a padded room. I screamed, yelled, and kicked the door. I wanted out! The window from the door was open directly in view of the nurses' station. I looked at them and yelled so much, they taped up the window with paper so they couldn't see me. They came in and strapped me down on a table. I was not in a straight jacket like you see in the movies, but I was on a gurney table and not able to move. I urinated all over myself because they

4

would not let me go to the restroom. Finally, after several hours, they let me out. I wasn't allowed any visitors unless approved by the doctor. I kept pulling the fire escape handle and setting off the fire alarm in the entire hospital. Every time I did, it cost the city of Alsip, Georgia $10,000 to come to the hospital and check things out. They were billing me! I had no idea. The only thing I could think of was that they were holding me hostage. The voices in my head were getting worse.

Several weeks went by of nurses pinning me down, sometimes on the floor, and injecting medicine into my hip. I had used up all of my energy and was completely drained from fighting with them. Finally, I was to the point where my family convinced me to start taking the medication orally. They were giving me things like Tegretol, Lithium, and Zyprexa. Major Mind Drugs! The medication was so powerful; it caused my speech to slur. I came down from a mania that was so high; I completely crashed after two days on the medicine.

My parents, sisters, and husband continued to visit me. I was in a daze. My sister, Denise, thought if she brought me makeup and put some on my face, that it would make me feel better. Nothing on the outside was what I needed at the time. I needed Jesus and had no idea how to find him. In the book of 1 Peter 3:4 it says the following: "Rather it should be that of your inner self, the unfading beauty of a gentle and quiet spirit, which is of great worth in God's sight." That bible verse tells me that no matter what you do to the outside of your body; God can only shine through the inside out.

The halls were as cold and blank as the people that were admitted there. Across from my room was a girl who had dark eyes with circles around them, dark hair, and pale skin. I found out she was a waitress at a local restaurant. She was skinny and had very little expression on her face. Her wrists told her story. Several slash marks of attempts of suicide was the reason for her admission. Another man down the hall was there for rehabilitation from alcohol and drugs. You could hear people all during the night talking out loud, screaming, and crying. Every time you heard a buzzer sound, it was the door of someone wanting to come in the hallway. The only way to enter that top floor was with approval from the nurses' station. It was as if it were a prison cell. One girl managed to escape when going down for an x-ray. I can't say that I blame her. The top floor of the hospital was not the penthouse suite. It was the pit hotel.

After a good six to eight weeks in the hospital, I was allowed to go home as long as I stayed medicated. I did not want to go home to my husband at the time, because the guilt was still there. I still had such a heavy weight on my shoulders. I asked to go visit my grandmother in Florida. I stayed with her for two weeks and then called Michael to please come and take me home. He came and got me, and we tried to sort things out but I knew that things would never be the same as they were once. It was almost like starting at ground zero and trying to rebuild the Twin Towers. It would take a miracle.

After about six months, I got a job and stayed on the medication for a while. I kept the diagnosis hidden under the rug, so to speak. The anxiety attacks started happening frequently out of nowhere. When we would have sex, I felt like Michael was smothering me. I felt like I couldn't breathe. I went to a counselor, and that's when I was told to tell my family about the date rape which happened when I was sixteen years old. The counselor thought it would be healing for me. It wasn't. It just brought back the pain of the onset that triggered Bipolar Disorder.

Chapter Two

It's Raining Cats and Dogs

Looking back on my life, I have to wonder what caused the bipolar disorder. Did I have any symptoms prior to the date rape in high school? Let's dig in and try to find out.

Growing up was very hard for me, not knowing how long we were going to live in one place. My mom was single, divorced, and raising three girls on her own from the time I was two until I turned age twelve. At two years old in 1970, my parents divorced. My mom, Carroll, raised me and my two sisters, Connie and Denise, on a single income. My dad, Gene, was the every other weekend dad. I had no idea until later years that divorce was so prominent within our family.

My mom said that before I was born and she married my dad, sometimes she and my sisters would eat grits three times a day because she didn't have money for groceries. She did not believe in welfare and food stamps, even though we qualified for them. There was a time in her life where she worked three jobs just to support us. She worked as a secretary in the day. She worked at a grocery store at night, and the nights she had off she sold Tupperware. We grew up on Kool-Aid, bologna sandwiches, and of course peanut butter and jelly. One year for Thanksgiving my sister, Denise, appeared before the classroom at school and told what she enjoyed on her plate the most for Thanksgiving. She said, "All we had was peanut-butter and jelly sandwiches." Although, we only had sandwiches we had each other. We had joy and didn't know we were living in poverty. My clothes were "hand me downs" given to me from my sisters. We didn't have a spiritual upbringing. We didn't have prayer around the table at meal time or bible study lessons. We didn't have God in our home. We were on our own. We never had the luxury of going out to eat at restaurants. We lived in a trailer and what we had was given to us. Usually my mom would work through all of her vacation time because we needed the extra money. However, one year my mom saved enough of her paycheck and drove my sisters and me to Ruby

Dawn Glaser

Falls in Chattanooga, Tennessee. We had a blast and got to see some of God's creation that normally families in our situation would never get to experience. At Christmas time, mom would let us circle a few things from the department store catalog. She would then go down and put the items on layaway to pay for them. I'm sure my dad paying her child support helped with things like that. However, back then her child support was minimal. My mom worked long hours and we fended for ourselves. We were content. We had food, clothing, and shelter. In the Bible, it says in the book of 1 Timothy 6:8 the following: "But if we have food and clothing, we will be content with that." God knows our needs and he provides for them.

Mom transferred with her job at the grocery store to Atlanta when I was age seven. I would make friends and then we would move, and I would have to start all over in a new school and make new friends. It seemed as though we moved often, and when we didn't move, I was not happy no matter where we lived.

I moved in the middle of third, fourth, seventh, eighth, ninth grade, and again when I was a senior in high school. How did I ever have any friends? Now don't get me wrong, most of the moving was my idea after age twelve. I moved back and forth between my mom and my dad. I wanted a family. I wanted them together. That was never going to happen, so I chose to experiment with living with each of them at different times.

What child doesn't want their parents together after a divorce? I never knew what it was like for them while they were married. They divorced when I was just two years old. For me I was shy, had low self esteem, and was just plain trying to fit in with the "in crowd" no matter where I was. I wanted a family. I wanted to be popular. I was searching. I was searching to fill a void that only Jesus could fill. If only I had known then what I know now, I just might have changed a few things. The year I turned ten years old my mom remarried and when I turned twelve my dad remarried. Wow! Now I've got two instant families. Wrong. Sure, I had two families, but was it like the perfect family you would see on television? Were they like the television show "Little House on the Prairie"? No.

My mom was always working around the clock. My older sisters got married in their late teens and moved out of the house. I was left with my stepfather who barely spoke a single word. He minded his own business, read the paper, went to work, came home, and watched baseball. We watched the Braves play, played basketball occasionally, bowled together, and fished together some. There wasn't much conversation. It was very rare that we ever did anything together as a family. I don't recall a time when my mother and I spent quality time together during my teen years. (That came later in life.) We never went to church. When I went to sleep most nights mom was working. When I woke up mom was already gone to work. I made my own breakfast, snacks, dinner, and washed my own clothes. She was literally never there.

I thought, "well why not try moving in with the father I really don't know?" He has a new wife now and maybe we can be a family. Before seventh grade started, I packed my bags and called my dad. There I was leaving my school and starting all over in a new one. I made friends quickly but hated my stepmother. She was very critical towards me, and jealous of the time I spent with my dad. She cursed, drank, and smoked like a freight train. I hated it all. She asked me if I was moving in with them to break them up. She resented me for some reason it seemed. I loved my dad's house. It was on five acres of land on a creek and was very peaceful there. The only way I found it though was stepping outside.

After I had put in my school year, I wanted out. I moved back in with mom again. I started skipping school and just not showing up. My mom never knew because she would leave for work early before I got out of bed. I just stayed home. When it came time for me to graduate eighth grade I learned that I had to go to summer school to pass. My mom took me and after summer school, I moved back to my dad's house. I'm not sure why this time. I may have been embarrassed about failing the eighth grade in front of my friends. Why did mom allow this? I have no idea.

When I moved to live with my dad, I did not get a warm reception from my stepmother, Becky. She seemed to persuade my dad to turn against me at times. I always felt like the red-headed stepchild. I felt like all she ever wanted out of me was to be her maid. She smoked, gossiped on the phone constantly, and cussed like a sailor. The whole house always smelled like an ashtray. I always felt like I couldn't get enough fresh air. She ordered me around and I felt like I was her puppet. She would tell me to clean the bathroom with a toothbrush and wash out the toilet with a wash rag instead of a toilet brush. She did the cooking and I did everything else. I resented her. She had a son from a previous marriage who was several years younger than me. Keith had no clue. He played with his "He-Man" action figures and kept to himself.

Becky always had a hateful tone in her voice and looked for fault in everything I did. I'll never forget the day I came home early from school because I was sick. Becky looked at me and said, "I bet you're faking it; you're not sick." I immediately threw up all over the carpet. My dad cleaned it up.

Becky would criticize my dad often and he would just get up and walk away. He never argued back at her. He let it go in one ear and out the other. I don't know why he never stood up to her. I think she treated me the way she did because she grew up with alcoholic parents. Becky would tell me not to tell my dad that she was taking us to her parents' house to visit. We would go over there, and the cops would be there. Her dad would be drunk and out of his mind. He was waving around a revolver and had thrown a chair out of the window of his home. Her mother drank and smoked, too. It seemed like her whole family did, (including her sister Emily and her family). None of them ever seemed truly happy. There was no joy in her parents' house. Her parents' house was one that was broken by alcoholism. I hated living with them, but I stayed because I found refuge in my friends at school.

Becky seemed friendly on the outside to those around her and occasionally we would have a few laughs here and there, but they were few and far between. We took a couple of family vacations, but as soon as we came back home everything was just the way it was before we left. She taught me how to cook and, of course, clean, but, for the most part the bad times outweighed the good. Out of the blue, Becky would start arguments with me and get right up in my face and dare me to hit her. I am glad that season of my life is over.

After 7th grade, I decided I had had enough of Becky and moved back to South Georgia. When I was thirteen years old and living with my mom, I went to a Christian concert at a football stadium with my sister Connie. The night air was crisp. The stadium was packed. The stadium lights were very bright. The music was phenomenal and the message seemed very clear when the gentleman spoke of God's son, named "Jesus". At the end of the event they asked all of us to hold hands and pray. "If there is anyone who would like to know that their name can be written in the Lamb's Book of Life and be with God eternally when you die, then come down out of the stands and repeat a prayer with me." the man said. My sister, Connie, squeezed my hand tight. She must have been praying for me. I immediately felt warmth come over me, and I started shaking and crying. I looked up and said, "I'm going down there." She went with me and I accepted Jesus as my Savior to come and be the Lord of my life that summer night in 1981. I then went to my local church, Holy Fire Baptist Church, in Lance, Georgia and was baptized within the next two weeks. I started going to church regularly with my sister and attended a Monday night youth Bible study. It was good, but after my sister graduated and moved out I was alone again it seemed, even though I had Jesus. I didn't have an accountable friend and Satan stepped into my life just as easy as he stepped out. Without my parents going to church and keeping me on track, I was lost again. Satan was about to take me on a roller coaster ride for the next twenty years until I would begin to understand the concept of the cross. I started staying out of school without my mother knowing and missed so many days that I failed the 8th grade. I was embarrassed and asked to move back to my dad's. My mom allowed me to go and soon, I was enrolling in yet another brand new school.

High school was not easy. It was fun, hard, and painful all rolled into one. I somehow made friends quickly. I had one very close friend named Millie that lived near me. We rode the bus together and hung out a lot. Her grandmother and my grandmother lived on the same road. We had fun. We would go to the skating rink on Friday nights. We would spend the night with each other and stay up the entire night. We would practice the moon walk to Michael Jackson's "Beat It".

I had another friend named Sherry, who told me she wanted me to meet someone. Before I knew it, at the age of fifteen, I went on a blind double date and was totally infatuated with the boy! That night I got in so much trouble. I told my dad I was spending the night with Sherry, and she told her grandparents she was spending the night with me.

Her grandmother called my dad and asked what time she would be home the next day, and we were caught! After riding around and drinking past midnight we met my dad in the driveway at 2:00 a.m.in the morning. We had the look of shock on our faces. The boys drove off, and I was totally grounded and got the worse whipping with a belt you could have imagined. Becky told him, if it was her, that her dad would have made sure she never did that again and would whip her. So, my dad did exactly that, and he had a hard time knowing when to stop. He hit me so continuously hard, that I crawled under my bed to get away from him.

The boy I was with was named Jeff and was very good looking. He had dark brown hair, brown eyes, and a quirky little smile. His football number was fifty- two. I knew everything about him. His birthday was January 29, and he liked Country Music. His favorite chewing gum was Big Red, but he also dipped Skoal occasionally. He was what most people called a true redneck country boy. I think I was drawn to him because he was what my dad wanted me to stay away from! I was head over heels and drawn in hook, line, and sinker. He was almost a year older so he would soon be driving. We were together all the time. He had a big Chevrolet truck with huge wheels, and we would go off- roading a lot. His parents owned the only local store hang-out in the one red-light town. They were known for money and whatever Jeff wanted, he got. He played football, and every Friday night when there was a home game, I would sit with his parents in the stands, watch the game, and cheer him on. We would stay after for the dance in the gym, and he would have me home by curfew. One time he brought me home early, and we fell asleep on our couch watching television. His parents called and woke my parents to ask if they had seen him. They found us both on the couch in each other's arms, and it was not a pleasant moment.

In the fall, his parents rented a coach bus and headed to New Orleans for the Sugar Bowl to see the Georgia Bulldog's football team play. They asked my parents if I could go and of course, the answer was no. I really thought I missed out on that opportunity. Living in a small town, you just don't get many chances to get out! They did let me go to a Georgia Southern football game to see Jeff's cousin play. We went to movies, out to eat, spent Christmas holidays together, and mostly just made out like any normal teenagers. He was my first love, and I was sure we were going to get married. He gave me all the love and affection I needed because there was not any from my dad and certainly none from my stepmother. I just knew he was the one. There was just one problem. God was not in the picture. I thought God would forgive me because I just knew we would get married someday. Wrong.

He turned out to be just like any other sixteen-year-old in America with hormones through the roof, and he totally used me to get the one thing he had on his mind.

When my parents found out we had gone too far in our relationship, they put an end to me dating him. They invited his parents over to discuss our relationship at the dinner table. I was so embarrassed; I got up and ran to my room. He, like any other boy, quickly found someone else and dumped me. How could he do this to me? Didn't I mean anything to him? No. He was after one thing and one thing only. He got what he wanted, and when he couldn't get it anymore, he went on to someone else. I really do thank God for unanswered prayers!

When I was sixteen years old, I found a job working at the mall at a pretzel shop. My dad bought me a car and taught me how to drive a stick shift. It was a yellow Datsun B-210. It was an ugly car, but I didn't care because it got me from point A to point B. I finally found the freedom I thought I was looking for in my life. I was able to go places on my own and get away from the criticism at home.

It wasn't long before I noticed another boy that really liked me, his name was James. He was a year older than me but didn't live very far away. He had a smile on his face all the time. We had an elective class together called "Middle East and Asia", and we sat beside each other in school. We double dated a lot with one of my good friends, Leslie. We went skiing on the lake. We went to concerts and out to eat. Then before I knew it, the relationship quickly ended.

He took me to the Junior-Senior prom. I wore a long pink dress with ruffles, white-lace gloves, and roses in my hair. I felt like a princess. He wore a white tuxedo with white tails. He rented a limo, took me to Red Lobster, and bought me flowers. He made me feel special. After the dance, the limo driver took us back to his house. James had one thing on his mind that night. Yep, he was just another boy who was out for sex. I refused to give in to him that night. I asked him to take me home and walked out.

Chapter Three

Sometimes the Fog is Thick

It wasn't long before my senior year in high school snuck up on me. I didn't have a boyfriend my senior year, and it was hard to see my old boyfriend with someone other than me. Then something happened. A new boy arrived at our school and he was very striking to me. I couldn't take my eyes off of him. He was tall with dark brown hair and brown eyes. I didn't know him very well, just his name. His name was Wayne. One Friday night I went to a football game, and there he was. He was singing a rock-and-roll song out loud and standing close to me. He glanced at me, and I glanced at him and smiled. We talked and he offered me a ride home. My girlfriend asked me was I sure, and I said, "I will be fine."

He didn't take me home. The radio was playing. The roads were dark. He asked me where I lived, and I told him. I thought that was where we were headed. He slowed down the truck, and I asked him if something was wrong. He made a turn on a dirt road of an open field that was pitch black dark. There was no one around. He turned off the truck and the lights and stared at me. I said, "What are doing?" He pinned me down on the floorboard of his black Ford truck during the act. He told me not to say a word to anyone. I felt like he was choking me the way he pinned me down. I couldn't scream. I couldn't breathe. I couldn't move. Afterwards, he drove me home, and I got out, went inside, and immediately took a shower. I had bruises on me. It was a horrible experience. The rape was an experience I will never forget. He treated me like a piece of garbage, and when he was done with me, he threw me out. I had no control. I was taken advantage of in the highest capacity and then afterwards, I was made to feel like the lowest of lows. I felt like the woman in the bible named, "Tamar". When Amnon raped her, he threw her out and was done with her. I had no idea how much one night could change the rest of your life, until that moment occurred.

I knew I couldn't say a word to my father because I thought he would have said something along the lines of it being my fault or that I had asked for it by getting him to take me home. My dad was always telling me how to dress, how much make up was too much, and how to wear my hair. My dad had to meet every guy I dated before I went out, and I had a curfew. Of course, I may have broken curfew a few times, but did I deserve this? No. I didn't deserve it anymore than any other young girl or woman deserves it.

If I had only known what would have happened that night I would have stayed home. This was the start of the rainstorm. It was a battle of my mind that was a traumatic experience that gave Satan a free ticket into my being. He stole my joy, and he stole my future. I wish I could warn girls today to keep their bodies respectful, and keep their virginity until marriage the way God intended. I would love to teach them to make wise choices and not be easily influenced as I was back then. If only I had known.

After that weekend, all I could think of was to escape. I called my mom, and she came and got me. I started over again in the middle of a school year. I graduated early in January 1986, and never got to walk with my class in June of that year. Satan laughed. I cried.

At the age of seventeen and out of high school, I found myself working at Wal-Mart, then as a waitress, in the mall, and at a drugstore. Where was I headed? What was my direction? I had none. I was not involved in church, lost touch with Jesus, and had no clue. I dated boys I knew from high school and one in particular that I had met from the skating rink years prior. I would never talk when we went out. I never knew what to say. Zach wanted me to open up to him more and I just couldn't bring myself to say hardly anything at all. I met his brother and parents. It seemed like he had a nice family, but I still had such low self-esteem that I couldn't move forward in a relationship. Satan was still laughing.

I remember that year my dad wrote many letters to me and I never answered one. I wanted to leave that part of Georgia in a jar with the lid screwed on tight and never go there again. It was painful, and to this day still is, somewhat. It's been twenty-six years ago, but the memory is still very vivid in my mind while writing this. Praise the Lord that He has erased the memory of my attacker's face.

Not only was I like Tamar, I was also beginning to become like the woman in the bible named "Rahab". I would date several guys and use them for instant pleasure. I didn't care if they had feelings for me or not. I wanted to feel loved, but didn't know how to love. Rahab was a woman who was a prostitute in the book of Joshua in the Bible. She later found faith and trust in God. She helped the Israelites spy on their enemies in Jericho, and in return God remembered her because of her faith and saved her and her family from destruction. It would be years ahead of what was to come before I would learn complete trust in God, and He would erase my slate clean.

If you are a girl or a woman and you have gone through a similar experience, don't lock it up in your mind for years like I did. Seek Godly counsel so that you will not blame yourself and consider it your fault. In this day and time, many women now speak up and contact the police right away. No means no, even if it's someone you know personally. No one has the right to violate you.

For the girls that are caught in a trap of thinking that sex is the only way you will ever be shown love, my heart goes out to you. Love is tender, and it was not intended by God to be used as a tool for an instant pleasure outside of marriage. True love waits. So many times I looked to boys and other men, but if only I had known the true love of my Lord and Savior, He would have shown me who he had chosen for me to spend eternity with. He never meant for me to choose on my own. He loved me enough to die for me and pay the penalty of my sin so I wouldn't have to. He did the same for you! John 3:16 it says, "For God so loved the world that He gave His only begotten son, that whosoever believeth in Him; should not perish but have everlasting life." God has all the love you'll ever need. If you are truly loved by someone else He places in your life on top of that, count your blessings.

Don't search for the rest of your life for love when Christ has already given it to you. His love, His life, through God's grace is sufficient. Pray for Him to bring you someone that is a believer of Jesus and walks in His pathway. Pray for God to send someone that will be a Godly man, loving husband, and Christian father. Pray that if the boy or man you are with right now is not that person for God to close the door on the relationship and open another one. God is all powerful and knew your plan before you were born, so let him be your compass and navigate you through the rough waters.

Chapter Four

Showers of Blessings

When I was seventeen years old I went to my sister, Connie's apartment to visit one weekend, and it just happened to be Father's Day weekend. She said, "We are planning to go to the lake for the day. Do you want to come with us?" "Sure," I said. Well, little did I know my brother-in-law at the time had called his friend, Michael on the phone and told him that he was going to meet his future wife. Michael told Thomas he couldn't because they were having a family meal and would catch up with him later. Thomas told him that if he changed his mind, we would be at the lake.

After we had been there an hour or so, this guy comes up with a Frisbee and starts talking to us. I pondered for a moment, trying to figure out who this guy was and how he came out of nowhere. It was Michael, and I fell for him immediately. We threw the Frisbee to each other and grilled out that day. We had a great time. When we got back to the apartment, he asked for my phone number, and I gave it to him. It was two whole weeks before he called me. He said he thought since I was four years younger, that I was too young for him. We set a date to go to a Mexican restaurant called Paco's. We got the food to go and went to Sioux Park for a picnic. It was a wonderful day of sunshine and laughter. We really hit it off and started from that day forward to have a wonderful relationship.

His family was awesome. To me they were the Norman Rockwell family. Michael came from a family of six children. His parents, Anna and Phillip, were middle class and both worked in the school system. They had Sunday pot roast dinners after church, played cards, board games, and sang Christmas Carols around the piano in December. They were the family I had longed for. They were the family that I saw on TV and would dream about having. Michael and I started seeing each other more and more until one day we decided to "live in sin" and moved in together. I was seventeen years old, and had moved out on my own into an apartment. We had very little money but had a lot of great times together. We lived on love and casseroles.

Michael's parents owned a place at the beach in Florida. Because it was only three hours away, we were there almost every weekend. We grilled out a lot, went to the park, and spent time with his family. Anytime there was a birthday or holiday it was a "big deal". Michael had a lot of nephews and nieces, and we enjoyed playing and babysitting with them. We would play baseball and basketball in the backyard for hours. We had just as much fun with them as I think they had with us. We would take all of the kids to different places and hang out. I loved all of them dearly. We had no desire to start a family right away. They filled that desire of having children, and we were content.

We enjoyed traveling even though we were always broke. We liked to go camping because it was cheap. We camped in Jennings, Florida and went tubing down the river. It was beautiful because the river was surrounded by underwater springs.

In our marriage, it seemed I was always making casseroles and we were eating at his parents. We lived around the corner from them and just got in

the habit of popping in anytime we wanted. They
didn't mind; they were like the "Cleavers" on the
television show, "Leave it to Beaver." "Come in
and have a seat!" We played Canasta, spoons, and
board games a lot. Some nights we would play
cards well past midnight. When it came out, we all
played Nintendo until the early morning hours. We
loved the" Dr. Mario" game. The only problem was
the music to the game would stay in your head for
days. It was a treat to play Canasta because Phillip
liked that game and would join in with us. Anna
loved games. She loved playing with all of her
grandchildren. We would play Scrabble, and she
would win. We would play Chinese checkers, and
she would win. We would play Othello, and she
would win. We would play Spades, and she would
win. There just wasn't any game that the woman
was not a master at!

If I had to choose a woman in the Bible for
Anna, I would choose Sarah. Sarah was the wife of
Abraham and the mother of Isaac. The name Sarah
in Hebrew is translated as one of high rank and
princess. Anna not only shined on the outside, but
her inner beauty was worth a thousand gems. To be
around her you knew you were walking on holy
ground. She feared the Lord. She was faithful. She
had many children and raised them the best she
knew how. I felt honored to call her mom. At
nineteen years old, to have a mother-in-law like her

was a blessing. She taught me so much about values and what it meant to have the Holy Spirit inside of you. She played the piano beautifully. At Christmas, we would sing together hymns which were so much fun. There was one time she and I sang together at a little church. She played, and we both sang the song "Freely". I will always keep that special moment dear to my heart. I will never forget her laugh. When she laughed everyone in the room lit up with a smile.

Thank you sweet Anna, for all of the gems you gave me to add to my collection. I will never forget you. In the book of Proverbs 31:25, it says the following: She is clothed with strength and dignity; she can laugh at the days to come. She speaks with wisdom, and faithful instruction is on her tongue. She watches over the affairs of her household and does not eat of the bread of idleness. Her children arise and call her blessed; her husband also, and he praises her; Many women do noble things, but you surpass them all. Charm is deceptive, and beauty is fleeting; but a woman who fears the Lord is to be praised. Give her the reward she has earned, and let her works bring her praise at the city gate. Anna, you have some hard shoes to fill. I can only hope that I can follow in your footsteps! Please forgive me for not measuring up as you hoped I would.

I thought I had gotten the instant family I had longed for, and it was a great feeling. I called his parents mom and dad, sometimes I had to pinch myself. We liked to play jokes on each other. I used to work for a doctor who had a cardiopulmonary mannequin. The hand was detachable. I took the hand and placed it in the ice bin of the freezer. When Anna reached in to get some ice for her tea, she slammed the door, screamed to the top of her lungs, and ran across the room in the opposite direction. I laughed so hard I cried! When she got her breath, she told me to never scare her like that again. She said she hadn't been that scared since her boys lived at home.

The whole family liked to play jokes on each other. One time Michael's sister, Cassidy, placed a plastic cockroach in Anna's bread bag when we were at the beach. Anna loved her fresh-baked homemade rye bed from a local bakery. One morning for breakfast, she pulled out the bread, reached in to grab a slice, and pulled out the cockroach. I think it scared her so badly she slung the whole loaf across the room! Another time Cassidy was staying over and getting ready for bed. Earlier in the day, I put a Styrofoam head under the covers with pillows lined up behind it to make it look like a real person. When she turned on the light, it looked like someone was in her bed. She screamed out loud, "Dawn!" We always loved to get a good laugh.

I scared Michael really badly one day. He was hanging curtain rods in our new house, and I was washing the dishes. He knew I was in the kitchen. I put ketchup on my hands, went running into the room where he was, and told him I cut myself. He was on a ladder and jumped off with a frightened look on his face. When I started laughing, he told me when I went to sleep that night, he was going to cut the power off to the house and scare me. Luckily he didn't. Good times!

Sometimes when Michael and I would just want to be by ourselves, we would go out in the middle of the night, sit, and look at the stars. One time we were in the middle of an open field called the "Kitchen Sink". That was the nickname for Vernon Park. The ground was so soft that it had become a huge sunken hole. It was below street level and as long as a football field. Years ago, the city had host their fireworks display there until it got too overcrowded. That night, we sat in a huge tractor tire for what seemed like hours just gazing at the sky and the moon.

Another time we took a blanket to the elementary school playground and just laid there looking up. We did things that were simple. We were so in love. One time he left a note on my car that read," Guess who loves you, the same person that cooked your dinner tonight." I went to his apartment, and he had made macaroni and cheese with canned tuna in it. It was hard to keep a straight face without cracking up laughing. We both ate it with a smile. I never told him how awful it was; instead I praised him for his effort.

One night Michael brought me some beautiful flowers. I asked, "Where did you get them?" He said he picked them from the hospital parking lot. It's a wonder he didn't get a ticket from a policeman for that! We used to go to a lake nearby called, "Lake Song". The local college would use the lake to practice sailing. Michael and I would sit by the sailboats on a boat landing, watch the shimmers of light dance on the water, hold hands, and talk for what seemed like hours into the night. It was so romantic.

During the Christmas season of 1987, Michael took me to the lake in town, and as we were sitting on a bench, he proposed to me. He slipped off a ring on my finger and slipped the engagement ring on in place of it. As we were all smiles and giddy, a lady came out of her house and literally cursed at us! What do you think y'all are doing out here? "Y'all are just disgusting," she said. I couldn't even say anything to the lady because I was still on cloud nine! What a day!

We planned a wedding date for June 18, 1988. It seemed fitting, as we had met in June around the same exact weekend two years prior. I wanted to get married in a church and have all of our relatives attend, so I asked my dad about it. He said that they didn't have a church they attended regularly. I suggested to him to find one, and he did. We were married at Grace Baptist Church in Alsip, Georgia.

My stepmother, Becky, loved to be in control and chose to plan the entire wedding as if it were her wedding, and upset my mother over the entire ordeal. I was only nineteen years old. I had no idea how to run a wedding and just thought it would be easier to say, "OK". I really don't resent Becky for the way she ran the show. I was just too young to speak up or know any better. Therefore, that is what I did. Unfortunately, I was so young and stupid, I had no idea how hurt my mother was at my wedding. I regret that for my mom, but in years to come I made sure she was definitely known as my one and only Mother.

We had both of our families there. My colors were burgundy, pink, and gray. It was fun to feel like a princess, but it only lasted an hour. Does anyone really remember our songs? Does anyone really remember our vows? Does anyone remember what my cake looked like? God does. He remembers every detail. We said our vows before Him, and we broke them. I was too young to know better. I know now what not to do. God keeps me grounded, and I will always put him first.

On our honeymoon, we drove to Lake City, Florida, spent the night at a hotel, and the next

morning we caught a plane out of Orlando, Florida
to the Bahamas. I'm not much for flying, so I was
scared to death! It wasn't a big jet plane. It was a
two seat puddle jumper over the ocean. I kept
waiting for the door to fly open any minute. I
embedded my fingernails into my seat and hung on
for dear life! When we got there, we had several
things go wrong. Our mopeds which we rented to
tour the island conked out on us. We had to pay
someone ten dollars just to tell us the spark plug
came loose. Then the lights in our hotel went
completely out due to a tropical rain storm. The
hotel staff brought us candles. It should have been
romantic, but it was scary at the thought of not
having any electricity on an island out in the middle
of the ocean! All I could think of was, "Lord, get us
home quickly!" I was not a happy camper! My
monthly friend was visiting to top everything else,
and I was one crabby chick!

On the way home from our honeymoon we were
driving on a major interstate and noticed that our
gas gauge wasn't working. Something was wrong
with the floater in the gas tank, and we had no idea.
We thought we had a full tank of gas when it was
actually almost empty and running on fumes.
When we pulled off the exit and got out, I realized
that I had locked the keys in the car. Great, what
now I thought. Michael laughed, leaned against the
car with his arms crossed, and made me go ask for

help. I found a coat hanger from a dry cleaner, and we managed to get back home in one piece, thank goodness!

That was an adventure for sure. One of my favorites though was when Michael and I went to California. His brother lived there, so we had a free place to stay. It was beautiful driving in Yosemite National Park and Big Sur near Monterey, California. I hate that I didn't have a Nikon back then as I do now! Yosemite had a waterfall called, "Bridal Veil Falls", and it was breathtaking. That would have been a great scrapbook.

I remember when we were traveling through Los Angeles we were pulled over by a policeman who told us to leave the area before dark due to gangs. It was not safe. There was a brown haze over the entire city when you looked down from Big Bear Lake. The air was thick and I knew I never wanted to live there. However, visiting Venice Beach was fun. It was entertaining to watch all the crazy people rollerblading and men with big muscles lifting weights on the beach. It was so hot and crowded everywhere you looked. Instead of enjoying people watching, I was worried about the people watching us!

One of the most memorable parts of the trip was when I had to go to the bathroom. We were riding in the back seat of Michael's brother's car driving up a mountain that was thousands of feet above sea level. When we arrived at the top, we went into a restaurant. I ran straight for the bathroom. The minute I got into the stall, there was not any toilet paper anywhere! I ran out, found Michael, and had the look of desperation on my face. He ran into the men's restroom and got a wad of toilet paper for me. With a million eyes staring at us, he handed it to me. I was so embarrassed. Michael was right though when he said, "Dawn, you will never see these people again." Thank the Lord!

We ventured down to Key West, Florida one time. I enjoyed touring Ernest Hemingway's house and eating at Crazy Jill's. It is an awesome place to view the sun going down on the water at dusk near Bridget Square. Several artists come out every day to perform. There was a juggler and a mime. The one that intrigued me though was a person painted silver from head to toe and dressed up like the Statue of Liberty. I wish I had pictures of it so I could share those with my son Preston. Someday he will just have to visit it himself. He would love the ice cream stand at the beginning of the seven mile long bridge. It was literally the best ice cream I have ever had. I loved the coconut! Sometimes the thought of the taste of that ice cream is so good, it takes me back.

Michael and I definitely enjoyed our sightseeing and travelling, but we had some weird experiences, too. There was one time when we were coming back from the beach on a country road. Four men were carrying a casket across the street to the cemetery from a church. We were going about sixty-five miles an hour and had to come to a complete halt in the middle of the road. Now, that's a sight you don't normally see two feet in front of you!

One time around Christmas, I heard a knock on the door. I answered it, as Michael was on the phone. A guy with a duffle bag started talking quickly about a new product he wanted to sell me. He said, "The product is called, "Watch This." As he was reaching in his duffle bag, Michael caught on to the guy, slammed the door in his face, and locked it. The guy took off running, and I was scared to death. I didn't do very well when fear came into the picture. I called the neighbors across the street and had them looking outside. I have no idea why we never called the police. We should have.

There were times I had anxiety attacks, and I think that was one of them. Other times when there were too many people around I would have one. I don't know why, but if I was in a house with more than ten people, I felt as if I couldn't breathe. I also found out that I was claustrophobic, which didn't help matters. All of that though seemed to derive from the high school date rape. Amazing how one moment of your life can leave you screwed up for years!

In the book of Romans chapter twelve, it says the following: "Do not conform to the patterns of this world, but be transformed by the renewing of your mind. Then you will be able to test and approve what God's will is; His good pleasing and perfect will." If only I had known to instill the word of God in my mind daily back then, I would have been able to fight off the enemy that was in my mind, my thoughts, and my dreams. Where Jesus is near, the enemy is not.

Chapter Five

Waves of Warfare

After my very first manic-depressive episode in the hospital, I finally went back to work after about a year of trying to find the right medication. I worked an eight-to-five job, and Michael and I had the weekends together. Things were okay, but not quite the same. I was still afraid of being attacked. I hated staying by myself and had wicked dreams that woke me up in the middle of the night trying to catch my breath. There were times I would wake up and feel the presence of someone standing over me, and I would scream to the top of my lungs. There were times I felt someone breathing in my face and I wanted to scream, but no words would come out.

41

Satan had a hold of me and this time he was choking me. For years, I would wake up in the middle of the night and hear a knocking noise as if someone was knocking on the door. It gave me chill bumps all over.

Do you ever wonder where fear comes from? My sister, Denise, told me years ago that in the book of Timothy it says that "God did not give us the spirit of fear, but of love, power, and a sound mind." (See 2 Timothy 1:7) If God didn't give it to us, it comes from Satan. He instills it in our brain from media, television, horror movies, and of course, people. If children never watch television, hear the sound effects, see others in fear, then don't you think they would never be afraid? I do. For me, though, it was spiritual warfare passed down. My mom slept with a gun when we were young. To this day, she is in her late sixties and still carries a gun with her. She was in fear for her life. I think just knowing that, I was in fear of being attacked for so many years. She passed down fear to me.

One night in the early 1970's while at a Tupperware party, a man was hiding in the back seat of my mother's car. He held a gun to her head while I sat watching in the front seat. She somehow talked him out of hurting her, and he got out of the car. God was definitely watching over us that night! Another time, mom told me that when she was closing the grocery store on a very dark night, a man jumped out from between the Coke machines and pulled a gun on her. She immediately pulled out her gun and pointed it at him, and he took off running. I think my mom's fear stemmed from her first marriage to Greg. He was abusive in the worst way. He emotionally and physically abused her. I have to believe that the reason she carried a gun years later was for protection, so that the horror was not repeated.

Mom worked at a grocery store that was open twenty-four hours; so when she wasn't at home, it was scary for me. One night when we lived in Dyson, my sisters told me they would be on the steps outside and for me to stay in the apartment. It was late at night, and I opened the door to see where they were. They weren't in sight. That was a very scary feeling, and I remember it as if it were yesterday. I don't know if it happened often or not. I always trusted what they told me. I remember staying with a girl named Michelle next door a lot. I even remember spending the night with her. I think my mom worked so much that she expected us to look out for each other in whatever way we were able.

While in Dyson, I remember my mom thought she heard something in the middle of the night. She aimed and pulled the trigger of the gun. It was my sister, Connie, sleepwalking. Denise yelled and saved her just in the nick of time from a real tragedy. It would seem that after that happened; my mom might reconsider having a gun under her pillow. She did not reconsider. The grip of fear that Satan had on my mom must have been intense. For years, she would take tub baths instead of showers. This was so that if someone broke in, she would be able to hear them coming and have time to defend herself.

In Proverbs 29:25, it says the following: "Fear of man will prove to be a snare, but whoever trusts in the Lord will be kept safe." That Bible verse makes me wonder how much Mom put her trust in the Lord back then. Did she know that in the Bible there are three hundred and sixty-six bible verses on the topic of fear? Did she know that God even gave us an extra one for leap year to fear not? The Spirit of Fear wreaks havoc in your mind once it's in there. It takes a lot of prayer and getting into God's word to overcome it. In my case, it took forty years.

My dad has a gun as well. He was in fear for his life. I do believe in protecting your family, but I also believe that God is our protector and no matter how we die, if we are a child of His, we will be in eternity with Him. There is no fear in that, my friend!

Spiritual warfare was something that never crossed my mind until my sister told me about it and, looking back now, it all makes perfect sense.

Satan wants you to never go to Heaven. God wants to have you, keep you as His child, and have you spend eternity with Him. It's a struggle. Satan tempts you. God redeems you. If only I had known back then what I know now I would have saved myself years of torment. How could I have known?

I also think spiritual warfare plays on your emotions. When my mom told me that she went into a major depression after her divorce, I knew Satan was attacking her mind. Satan had her right where he wanted her until one day she just snapped out of it. I would like to think someone was praying for her, and God gave her the rope to pull herself up and out of the pit.

I wish I would have grabbed a hold of that rope as my mom did. I had terrible anxiety attacks that seemed to get worse. They happened frequently while surrounded by people. I had what the psychiatrist would call Social Phobia. I also was claustrophobic paranoia around people, and had trouble with speech. Could all of this have been Bipolar Disorder? I had very little self-esteem and felt the need to be noticed, to get recognition, and to be creative in order for people to like me. I needed Jesus. Where was He? Little did I know He was there all along just waiting for me to knock on the door and ask Him into my life. I had so much insecurity even though I was married to a great guy. I had a nice home, husband who loved me, a dog named Jesse, and I was lonely inside. I still craved attention and someone to notice me. I had a great family and great in-laws, but felt I was missing something. I wanted to fill the void. I was so confused. Satan was controlling me, and I had no idea.

Who would have thought that the enemy of all lies was telling me lies, and I believed them. Even though other people would tell me that I was pretty or funny, I always thought they were just being nice. I never believed them. I told myself that I could never measure up, was overweight, could not carry on a decent conversation with anyone, and would never get that raise due to lack of knowledge. Satan had a way of attacking my thought life!

For instance, when I was younger and lived with my dad and my stepmother, I was in a world of criticism. I could never please her with anything I tried to accomplish. I tried out for cheerleading. She drove me there but sat in the car and never even came in the gym for the support that I so desperately needed. When I found out that I didn't make the team it was the worst let down ever. She said something along the lines of "I told you so". I never got up the courage to try out again. How many girls were like me? Did they try out with high expectations, only to be shot down immediately by a flaming arrow from the enemy? I was, and I didn't have God's word to defend myself. He tells us to put on His armor. In the book of Ephesians 6:10-11 it states: "Finally, be strong in the Lord and in His mighty power. Put on the full armor of God so that you can take your stand against the devil's schemes." If I had only had the word of God within me, I would have been able to take a stand. Instead, I retreated into my shell a scared little girl who let Satan attack me from all angles. If you are a young girl who never thinks that you can measure up to the cheerleading squad, please know that God is your biggest fan.

God sent His Son to die on a cross for you and stretched out His arms as far as the east is from the west to show you how much He loves you. Never let Satan get a foothold, as it says in Ephesians 4:27 or you will already be defeated. You are beautiful just the way you are. Please don't let anyone tell you differently. Get a mirror and stare at it for as long as you can. I did this once at a women's conference and it was the hardest thing I had done in a long time! The pain, the hurt, the insecurities, and low self-esteem were all there looking at me. However, after those thoughts lifted the Lord spoke to me and said, "You are beautiful, just the way you are, and that's why I only made one you." I've since forgiven my former stepmother, and I am thankful for the good things she taught me such as how to cook and clean, and I can now focus on those. I wish I was able to see her years ago

Dawn Glaser

through the eyes of Jesus and let her know that He
loves her. If I had, I would have been able to show
her His Holy Spirit and maybe help turn our
relationship around.

Chapter Six

A Storm's a Brewing

Michael and I were doing okay in our home in Lance, Georgia for a while until his payroll checks started to bounce. He worked for a family-owned business that could not stay afloat. He called his brother in Atlanta, and Austin suggested that we come and live with his family in order for Michael to get a job near them. Next thing I knew, I was turning in my notice at work and we were moving. I left a great job, my mom, and friends behind. I remember one of my friends said, "Why don't you just say no to your husband?" At the time, "No" wasn't in my vocabulary.

We lived in Austin's basement for just a few short months, and then it happened. I found out I was pregnant. I worked for a doctor in Ellijay, Georgia at the time, and I remember wondering after taking the pregnancy test how in the world we were going to survive. I took a book about being a father to Michael's work and handed it to him without saying a word. He must have thought something along the lines of, "What now, Lord?" His paycheck was not going to get us out of the basement, so he started going back to school to get a degree. We moved into an apartment and that's when everything went haywire.

He was going to school at a local technical college. One day he walked by a classroom and noticed that the class was laughing and having so much fun, that it drew his attention. Next thing I knew he was no longer in electrical engineering. He was now into Hospitality Management. He got a job at a prominent hotel chain working nights. He went to school during the day, and we never saw each other. We argued a lot. The fun had faded.

The love was dim, and I was miserable. I have to believe that he was too. Neither one of us had God in our lives. We did not have Him as the head of our household. We were not serving Him. Our marriage of nine years was crumbling.

In May of 1995, I gave birth to a beautiful nine pound twelve ounce baby boy who we named Preston David. Michael had just started a brand new job. The day Preston was born; he came to the hospital but did not stay with me overnight. He worked. After the family had come and gone, I had never felt so alone. I was in so much pain. I stayed five nights in the hospital. I remember a nurse tried to comfort me, but the pain was unbearable. I went home, and my mother-in-law came for two weeks. I was grateful to have the help but she could not mend the deep pain within me. After she left, my best friend Julie came for two weeks to help me take care of Preston. She was just like a sister to me, and I love her to this day. I cried the day she left and wondered, "Now what?" She helped me out in one of the worst times of my life that should have been the happiest.

Michael started working more and more. He was gone at all hours of the night. He would tell me that he was going to his brother's to get help with math. He wouldn't come home until after midnight sometimes. He would say he was going out for coffee after midnight when we had a coffee pot in our kitchen. He would say he lost track of time at the Pancake House while reading the paper. Where was my husband? Where was the father my son needed? Our family was falling apart just like a hem coming unraveled on a dress.

Not having any family near me made things worse. My mom was close to four hours away, and even though we called each other often, she couldn't take away the hurt. There is something about your mom hugging you and telling you everything will be all right, but this time she couldn't fix it.

If only we had put God first in our lives, I know things would have been different. My son was caught in the crossfire. He didn't have a choice. He didn't have a voice. Divorce was around the corner, and Satan was waiting to make sure it happened. He is the master planner of destruction, depression, divorce, and will leave you destitute! Lamentations 1:16 states: "This is why I weep and my eyes overflow with tears. No one is near to comfort me, no one to restore my spirit. My children are destitute because the enemy has prevailed." We allowed Satan to come into our home, and when we did, he took over and destroyed everything we had worked for, loved, and cherished. He is the father of all lies and we believed him.

Chapter Seven

The North Wind Came With a Vengeance

Michael started working day and night, which meant that Preston and I were left home alone. I was lonely, depressed, and just plain tired of the life we were living. I had very few friends. My family lived far away. It was almost like having a husband in the military only mine was working thirty minutes away. He continued to work nights and go to school in the daytime, and it was taking a toll on our marriage. We lived in apartments that were based on a sliding scale income. They were somewhat like government housing. They were nice, but when you looked out your window at night, things were very dark and the police were always patrolling our apartment complex. We lived in a three-level apartment building that had a lot of stairs. The people below us hated all the noise we made so they would bang their broom handle on the ceiling to quiet us down. It's hard to quiet down a vibrant two year old. Sometimes I would get so mad I would take my broom and hit the floor back. We now had a band going every night!

I began typing on the computer and making friends online. That's when he showed up out of nowhere. His name was Nick, and he was from up North several states away. He made everything sound so wonderful. He kept me up nights, and I was flirting with disaster. I heard his voice on the phone. He sounded so charming. Have you ever heard that Satan is a good-looking man? If only I had known my Savior back then. I listened to his every word. I used to wait up for Michael to go to work, now I couldn't wait until he left. He was manipulating me and I had no idea.

This man bought me airline tickets. I was foolish enough to travel to meet him. I didn't care, because he made everything sound so good. He knew my desires, my fantasies, my favorite places, my favorite foods, and my favorite songs. He was orchestrating my divorce. He was brainwashing me. Michael and I moved to a different apartment. Soon after we moved we set a court date for the divorce. Nick was so clever he called me the day of the divorce and told me exactly what to say, what not to say, and how to contact him when it was over. Michael put his wedding ring on the counter and left for work one day, and then it hit me. What have I done? I was in a whirlwind of disillusionment. This man got to me. Why? How could this happen? Why did I let it happen? A few months had passed and I broke things off. I told Nick I could not continue our relationship. That's when it happened again. I met someone else online in a chat room. This time, he was gorgeous!

I arranged to meet Chris with a friend of mine at a bar in a town called "Deer Run". This was definitely my "Pre-Jesus Days" as I call it. We immediately hit it off. The chemistry was there. He brought me roses the following weekend and took my son and me to the park nearby. We started dating. He was finishing college. The weekends Michael had Preston we went out to clubs, and I was drinking and living it up! Staying up late and not eating, I was getting very sick. My neurotransmitters in my brain were going haywire again.

I was Chris's first love. I was his very first girlfriend to take home to meet his mother and sister. From the moment I walked in their home, both of them never took their eyes off me for a second. I felt like they were judging me before I went before the jury. They were nice, but I could feel the worry in his mother's eyes. Chris made me feel so special. He was totally in love with me and I was on a roller coaster ride that felt so good! He was ready to marry me. We would go to the mall and window shop for wedding rings. Honestly, I think if he had the money he would have bought me one. We would go in a dress shop, and I would try on a dress for him. I would come out of the dressing room and his eyes were totally focused on me alone. We would go out to eat and sit in the same seat next to each other in a booth. We went to the movies. We were having so much fun together.

Chris loved Preston from the moment he saw him. He told me that when he saw me on the computer teaching Preston the alphabet, he knew he wanted to spend the rest of his life with me. Chris was majoring in computer technology at a local college. All of this was fun, but I was still living in a fantasy world. I was not eating or sleeping. I was losing weight tremendously fast. I was going in a downward spiral, and Chris was just a victim. He thought I was living a normal life. He had no idea anything was wrong with me, but one of my girlfriends noticed. Little sleeping and a lot of alcohol will make anyone do crazy things!

My friend, Linda, could tell I was talking unusually fast. She thought I was on drugs. She was wrong. She knew Nick, because the very first time I met him, she flew with me to meet his best friend. She called him and said, "Dawn is sick, come get her." He was in Boston at the time of the phone call. He left his job and drove non-stop all the way down to Atlanta to get me. He arrived, and I was so far gone. He asked me to marry him. I thought it was romantic for him to drive all that way for me. Stupid as I was I said ok. Next thing I knew I was packing and moving to Maine! Not only was I moving, I was dragging my son with me, who at the time was only two years old! That was crazy. Yes! It was totally insane to say the least! I had a great job, so I thought. I was in medical billing working for a neurosurgeon making close to fifteen dollars an hour. Nevertheless, I was less than six months divorced. I was seeing another guy who was absolutely in love with me. I didn't care. It was all pure fantasy!

Chris showed up at my door, and the apartment was empty. He didn't know what happened to me. He had no idea anything was wrong with me. It was Satan. He was telling me lies. I believed all of them! In John 8:44 it says: "When he lies, he speaks a native language, for he is a liar, the father of all lies." I did not have Jesus at that time. He was waiting for me, watching over me, and I didn't have a clue. I was headed straight on the pathway to the pit hotel, and I didn't need any luggage. It was almost as if I were in a trance, just shook my head and said, "Okay".

I called my family, told them where I was, and that I was fine. I thought I was fine, but I wasn't. I was in Maine six long weeks. During that time, I became pregnant. I got married to a man I barely knew outside the Internet. I had met his family. They all seemed very nice. He had a son named Carl, from a previous marriage, who was fourteen-years old at the time. He was tall, had brown hair, and dark eyes. He was your typical teenager. He liked girls, fishing, and playing soccer. Nick was tall, at least over six feet and had blue eyes and gray hair. He was eight years older than me. Nick had a small house. He worked a truck route and made close to sixty thousand dollars a year. In 1997, that was a lot of money to me. He didn't have much of it though because he spent everything he had on having fun: new truck, going to the ocean, eating out, and blowing everything he had while not saving anything. He was not saved and did not have a relationship with Jesus. He was Catholic. He was an altar boy when he was younger. He had no idea what it was like to have a relationship with Jesus. However, at the time I didn't either. Perfect match, so I thought. Boy was I mistaken!

Nick loved to travel, camp, fish, hike, and he loved the ocean. He made everything seem like an adventure! We would go crabbing and then have a crab boil. We would go camping on the beach and shoot off fireworks. We watched wild horses running on the beach. We would go hiking on trails from the Civil War that intrigued me. He would take me to beautiful scenic shops on the Barista Bay in a town called St. Vincent's. Looking down one of the cobblestone streets all you could see were shops on both sides. At the end of the street, you could see the bay with sailboats. It was a beautiful town. I loved everything about Maine in the summer and fall. It had a lot of history, green grass, and the ocean very close by. Nick knew I had a thing for antiques and would bring me home things I collected. One time we walked into an antique shop and there was a pickle jar filled with skeleton keys. I asked the owner if there was any way that there might be two of the same. She said she doubted it but we looked anyway. We turned over the entire jar on the counter and there were two keys that matched. We bought them and put one of each on our key chains. He would watch movies with me that I loved. He would point out historical places and discuss history. We would slow dance outside after midnight under the stars.

Nick's mother and sister made me feel welcome into their family. They would invite me over for tea in the afternoons. His mother would invite us over for dinner a lot. Still, I'm sure that deep down they thought, "Where in the world did this girl come from?" How did she just uproot her family and leave everything behind? I'm sure my family was thinking the same thing.

There was never a dull moment and we always had something to do or some place to go until one day when the bills started coming in. I thought to myself, this is real, and this is not a fantasy. Why am I here? How did I get here? I was on a manic episodic high in full swing, and I had just crashed. I would open the curtains to the window of Nick's small house, look out, and all I could see day after day were gray clouds. There wasn't any sunshine anywhere. It was cold in the dead of winter, and I saw no hope in sight. Nick would come home from work, and I would stop talking. He would ask what was wrong with me. I was homesick. I was waking up to a reality of confusion. He tried to buy me gifts to make me happy, but nothing helped. I was in a trance of despair. Instantly, I went into a deep depression. I had lost my husband. I lost his family, who I had adored. I had lost my job. I lost my friends. It was cold outside. It snowed and snowed every day for weeks. It was gloomy. I needed my mom. She was miles away.

I missed my grandmother and kept reflecting on how I spent my summers growing up at her house. It was so peaceful there, like a slice of heaven on earth to me. Would I ever find that kind of peace of mind that I longed for? My grandmother lived alone for over twenty years after my grandfather passed away. They had been married for fifty-two years and had six children. Her first born son died at birth. She never talked of that tragedy and kept the hurt and anguish inside her very soul. What a legacy! They made their home seem so welcome. They never argued. They laughed often. It was peaceful to me to be there. I loved every minute of it! In the book of Joshua 1:8-9 it says the following "Do not let this Book of the Law depart from your mouth; meditate on it day and night, so that you may be careful to do everything written in it. Then you will be prosperous and successful. Have not I commanded you? Be strong and courageous. Do not be terrified; do not be discouraged, for the Lord your God will be with you wherever you go." To me they lived the life that God had planned out for them. They honored God with prayer, obedience, and love. He blessed their home and their marriage to pass down a legacy for their children and children's children. She was a Proverbs 31 kind of woman. Would I ever be able to walk in her footsteps?

The day my world starting crashing was when I found out I was pregnant. Reality had just knocked down the door and said, "Hello". I think Nick was glad that I was pregnant. Looking back, I have to think that was his plan in order to keep me up there. He probably never thought I would have left since I was pregnant. Looking back, I'm surprised that I did leave. I was now most like the woman in the book of 1 Kings in the bible named "Bathsheba". She was an adulteress who became pregnant.

My emotions had gone from elation to depression in a matter of days. I didn't know what to do. I called my friend Julie that I worked with in South Georgia. She was my very best friend and like a sister to me. Twenty years later, we still keep in touch. She's a friend that even if you haven't spoken for years and you finally do talk, you just pick up where you left off. I knew she had money and could wire me some to come home. There was a bank across the street. She deposited five hundred dollars and I walked over and withdrew it immediately.

Nick went to work one night and I knew I had very little time because he would be calling soon. He called, and I tried my best not to let on what I was doing. His son Carl was with us, and he was asleep. I started loading up my car with as much as I could. I left Carl a note to call his grandmother who lived less than five miles away when he woke up if his dad was not back. I said that I was sorry, because I know it must have devastated him when he found that note. I barely had room for Preston in the car, and the next thing I knew I was driving out of Maine and into Virginia. It was amazing that our car didn't break down on the side of the road. So many things could have gone wrong.

I stopped in Richmond in the middle of the night and got a few hours sleep at a roadside hotel. It's a wonder we both were not kidnapped and killed! God was really watching over us. Like any two-year old, Preston woke up early and was hungry. I got up, checked out of the hotel, and started driving straight for Atlanta. I then stopped again and stayed at the hotel where Michael was working. I remember I couldn't sleep. I went across the street to a store to get Tylenol pm, and it barely phased me. What was wrong with me? Why couldn't I sleep? My mind was racing with thoughts that I couldn't control. I was running and scared. Satan had a tight grip on me and he wasn't letting go. I got in the car the next morning and drove straight to my mom's house. I remember when I got there I was shaking so and couldn't stop. It was as if I had downed a bottle of pills. I had only taken two Tylenol PM pills and that was it!

In a matter of six weeks, I had made a huge mistake that would leave a scar on me forever. What now? I talked to my friend, Julie. She asked me if I was I going to keep the baby. I said, "I don't know what I should do." She said that she knew where I could go and "take care of it". It would be easy and she would take me, but of course, it would be my decision. It was kind of like in the New Testament when Pilate knew it was wrong to crucify Jesus, he left it up to the people to decide so he wouldn't have any guilt in the future or be tied to any wrong doing. That way, Nick would never have ties to me, and I could end the relationship for good. I asked my mom what to do. She said it was up to me, and that she would not help me make that decision. I thought about it for what seemed like a week. I thought that if I didn't go through with it, I would always have a connection to Nick up north and could never regain my life back. God would forgive me. No one would know. I would just say that I had a miscarriage, and this part of my life would be a closed chapter.

I called my friend, and she drove me two hours away to a clinic I now will call Hell. I remember going in, and she waited for me. I signed some papers, and they told me to get undressed. The smell was of Clorox everywhere. The walls were gray. The countertops were grey. The chairs were black. This was Hell, and I knew it. They asked me to put on a hospital gown and come into a group session room. It was a small room. It had grey walls just like the waiting room. There was nothing colorful about this place. It was full of teenage girls! We were all in a circle. Gloom filled the air. The nurse asked me to fill out a form as to why I did not want to have this baby, and why was I considering "abortion". I didn't know what to write down. Had I really thought this through?

As the forms were handed out, I listened as the girls ahead of me were answering this so called, "advisor". So, what is the reason for coming in today, and why are you deciding to terminate the pregnancy? One girl stated, "Financial reasons". They asked the next girl the same question. Her answer was the same. When it came time for me to answer, I just casually said the same as well. How easy it is to terminate a life! There was no counseling. There was no, "Are you sure you want to do this?" Are you sure you have thought this through?" All you needed to do was make up one bogus statement, sign the dotted line to release them to put you on a table and do a procedure that is called "murder" in God's eyes. In the Bible in the book of Mark 10:9, it says the following: "You know the commandments: You shall not murder, you shall not commit adultery, you shall not steal, you shall not give false testimony, you shall not defraud, honor your father and your mother." I was a liar, a person who committed adultery, and a murderer. I now truly needed a Savior to redeem me from the pit of Hell. I needed Jesus, but He would not be found anywhere in that place for sure!

How could I have done that? How could I let my family down? How could I even consider something so casual but yet so cruel? Satan had a hold on me. He was now coming to kill! A man with a mask came in the room with his assistant.

He looked at me and never said a word. His assistant said that it would only take a second, and it would all be over soon. She held my hand, and I gripped it as hard as I could as a suction noise sounding like a vacuum cleaner started getting louder in my ears. The pain was excruciatingly horrific! There was some medicine that was supposed to help, but it couldn't even ease the amount of pain that I went through. I screamed as loud as I possibly could, and just like that, it was over. The assistant helped me to another "holding facility". This time it was so I could recover from what I had just gone through. I had to stay a certain amount of time so they could make sure I wouldn't pass out. After what seemed like an hour or so, my friend drove me to my mom's work. It was a long ride as we sat in silence. When we arrived at my mom's antique shop, I walked through the door, took one look at my mom, and hit the floor. I went down cold and was out like a light. My friend went and got me some of her Mountain Dew and poured it in my mouth. I awakened and felt so sick and weak. Being a nurse, Julie said that I probably lost a lot of blood. I knew that I had lost much more.

Somewhere between right and wrong, I lost a child that I would never know. In the Bible in the book of Jeremiah 1:5, it says the following: "Before I formed you in the womb, I knew you. Before you were born, I set you apart. I appointed you as a prophet to the nations." The Lord knew my child before it even had a chance. It had a heartbeat, but I did not allow it to continue beating. I regret that day of hell in my life. I had other options. Not a one ever crossed my mind long enough for me to consider. So many women are barren and want a child. I could have given the baby to someone wanting to adopt. No one sat me down and even asked me to reconsider or tell me my options. I had no support and I was without an accountability partner. Just like with what happened to Bathsheba, I lost my baby. God allowed it to happen. I wouldn't find out until later that just like Bathsheba, I would be redeemed and forgiven. God had adopted their baby and took it to Heaven and He did the same for me.

I went to my local church and pleaded with God to please forgive me. I now felt like the woman in the book of Mark in the Bible. When Jesus walked through the crowd, she knew that if she could just touch his cloak she would be healed. She touched him, and her faith healed her. I know that in my heart, He has since forgiven me, and I will see my child in Heaven some day. For that, I am grateful.

What young girls or women don't consider is the emotional trauma that comes with such an experience. Every time someone mentions abortion, you wonder how you could have done such a horrible act. Every time you get behind a pro-life bumper sticker, you think that Satan is reminding you what you have done. Every time you hear someone having a miscarriage and how distraught they were with what they went through, you feel guilty. Every time you hear of someone who has infertility issues and can't have children it makes you just sink inside at the thought of them finding out about my skeleton in the closet. It's taboo. You don't talk about it, but I plan to change that. I am breaking the chains to show young girls the torment I went through in hopes of saving their life!

However, after talking to some teens today, I realize that several of them think of abortion as a casual quick fix. No one ever tells them that they will have to live with the decision for the rest of their life. No one tells them that Satan will use every opportunity to bring it up and stab them with the pain they once felt as a reminder. I will never know if I had a little girl or a boy. I called that clinic a few years back to try and backdate it and have them pull the records to tell me. They could not locate my records. It's just the same. You see, Jesus wiped the slate clean for me as well. According to the book of Corinthians, He keeps no records of wrongs. I long for the day when I get to Heaven and can see the child that Jesus nurtured for me. I am thankful that God has washed me white as snow and that I am forgiven through Jesus. He gives me hope, and that's what I want to give back to other women through my story. If I can play just a small part in the redemption of someone else's story, then I will feel like I've accomplished something.

Two years ago, I went through a program called "Healing Hearts". You can go to www. healinghearts.org for more information if you need help as well. You can seek counseling through your local pregnancy center for the county you reside in. I am grateful for the woman who called herself "Vashti". She helped me get over the loss of a baby that was mine. I now know that I will see my child in Heaven someday. For that, I am grateful. In the book of Esther 1:11 it says: "to bring before him Queen Vashti, wearing her royal crown, in order to display her beauty to the people and the nobles, for she was lovely to look at." Thank you Vashti for sharing your crown of knowledge with me and restoring my soul.

Nick called for weeks after I moved back in with my mom. He asked her about the baby. She told him that there wasn't a baby to discuss, either it had been terminated or that I had a miscarriage. I have no idea. He never contacted me again. I filed for a divorce which was a six-week mistake. He finally gave up and signed the papers. It almost makes me think of the years in the 1940's when you would hear of mail order brides. I was an email-order bride who woke up and realized my home was in Georgia.

I can't imagine how things got so mixed up in my life during that time. I honestly toss it all up to Satan. He had a plan to destroy me, and he had me almost at the end of my rope. Years have passed, and I have blocked a lot of my memory. I am thankful Preston was so little that he doesn't remember any of that drama in my life. I don't know where Nick is today or what is going on in his life. I wish him well, and as with anyone, I truly hope he has found Jesus.

Chapter Eight

After the Rain

There I was, a woman who was back at home with her mother, and this time I had lots of emotional baggage with me! I needed a fresh start in my life. I needed my mom. I came back with not only my son, but I came back a basket case. I had, just in a matter of six months, gotten a divorce, gotten pregnant, moved North, married a man I hardly knew, lost a child, and hit the lowest of lows in the deepest, darkest pit I could have ever imagined.

What happened to me? I couldn't even look at myself in the mirror. I didn't want to talk to anyone or see anyone. I had no hope. I had no joy in my life. I didn't want to live. I wanted to die. However, I knew I had a son to raise so I felt trapped. I went to the altar steps of my home church where I was saved at age thirteen and begged God for forgiveness. I immediately went into a shell and into a deep dark depression. For almost a year, I lived with my mom and did nothing. I became an emotional eater and gained weight. I was on medication again for mental confusion and began to have nightmares. I would wake up in the middle of the night and see ghostly figures in my room. I would call my mom in there and of course, she saw nothing. What was happening to me?

I told my psychiatrist what I was experiencing, and instead of him thinking it might be a side effect of the medication, he just increased my dosage! I had no will, no motivation, and felt like I was just going through the motion. I would sit down at my mom's pond on her fifteen-acre property and just get lost in the stillness of the water. I wasn't talking much. I had no hope left in me. I didn't take care of myself. I wasn't functioning normally. I had lost touch with who I was and what my role was in life.

Finally, one day my mother had had enough. She came in my room and said, "The pity party is over." You need to get a job and get your life back! Not only did that hurt, but I knew that she meant it. I had a son that looked up to me, and I was in a pit with no way out. I started reading my Bible. I started going back to church. I got a job. I worked at the local hospital in the collections department. I started taking my son to a church preschool. Just like that, things started to look up again. My mom was right. She could not look at me anymore the way I was, and I could not even look in a mirror. I had become a woman whom I was ashamed of and did not know.

Who was Dawn anyway? Where did she go? When people say, "Oh you have no idea what I've been through or my past", I often think yes, but you have no idea what I've been through either. I have to think yes, I'm sure I don't know and yes, there is always someone out there who has it ten times worse than I do. My past had a tale that was so dark; it's amazing I was able to see a flicker of hope. At that point in my life I could not see because I was drowning in my own tears. I admired my mom through it all, raising three girls on her own for a while. If she could do it, then so could I.

I started going to church often and went to single outings with my sister, Connie. Then I met a guy named Gavin. He was attractive, and he went to church. I thought that since he went to church then things may just be okay. However, he was just another Wayne that preyed on single women at church because it was easy. He cussed often and although he tried to be nice to me and bring me flowers, I couldn't bring myself to fall for him totally. We dated for a few months. He took me to a football game one night and got so involved in the game that he began cussing at the opposing team with me sitting beside him. I got up and left the game without him. He kept calling me, and I thought I would never get rid of him.

It just goes to show that everyone who goes to church does not go for the right reasons. Looks can be deceiving and so can your heart. In Jeremiah 17:9 it says: "The heart is deceitful above all things and beyond cure." Who can understand it? I was letting my heart lead me. When was I ever going to learn to lead my heart? My heart was an open target for anyone who wanted to enter into it except God. He had been knocking on it for years. He was waiting for me to invite him in to my heart. Instead, I chose to let men into my heart, it was getting trampled on, and losing precious beats in the process.

Chapter Nine

God Sent Some Sunshine

In 1998, Preston and I had moved into an apartment of our own. Our groceries consisted of macaroni and cheese, cereal, and hot dogs. I had a black and white television and one gold couch. I had a table and a couple of chairs. We got by. It was hard, and I was struggling, but we were surviving. Michael had invited me to his parents' house for Christmas, and I accepted his offer. I thought to myself that there may be a chance that we could start over. When I walked in his parents' home, immediately I started to cry. It wasn't the same. I felt like an outcast. I had destroyed everything that God had given me. It wasn't the same, and I had to leave. My mom always said," Once you leave and burn a bridge, you can never go back". She was so right.

The following Saturday I went to my mom's house to visit. I don't know why I went to the mailbox for her, but I did. In the mailbox was a letter addressed to me. It was from Chris. He said in the letter that this one would be his last. He had been writing me letters every week for an entire year, and I had no idea. My mom had kept the letters hidden from me just like something from a movie! He said that if I thought there was ever a chance for us to please call him and left the number for me to call. He told me he had loved me from the moment he laid eyes on me and had never stopped.

I thought about it and called him. The very next weekend he drove down to see me with a dozen red roses. We picked up where we left off, only this time I was sober and on medication. I thought that too much time had passed between us, but once our eyes connected the chemistry came right back. We had a weekend love affair for a few months, and then Chris said that he couldn't continue driving down so far and wanted us to move in together in Atlanta. I looked at my crummy life, how broke I was, and how I was not going anywhere. I immediately said yes. Thinking back, I can pretty much bet that my mom did the same exact thing in her situation with my dad. It's funny how generational patterns work like that.

My mom had a talk with Chris and told him there would not be any other children from me, and that I would be on medication forever. She wanted him to make sure that he could live with that. Next thing I knew we were driving in a u-haul truck up the interstate headed north on Interstate 75. We moved into an apartment. Things were going okay I guess. I had a job. I enrolled Preston in preschool.

Chris was working nights a lot. There was something missing though. We weren't married. There wasn't a commitment. His mother would not even set foot in our apartment. She didn't want her son to have anything to do with a woman who broke her son's heart. It probably didn't help that I was older and had been married and divorced. I had no family nearby. This was going to be a struggle. The Bible clearly says in Corinthians 6:14 "Do not be unequally yoked together with unbelievers." I was saved, and was not following Christ. Was Chris saved? No. At that point and time in his life, he was not.

We were about to be in a world of hurt. I made another choice that I thought I could control and change on my own. I was wrong. I thought that I would be able to save myself and save Chris. What was I thinking? Was I trying to play God? I certainly wasn't letting God control my life. I thought I knew. I would marry Chris and then I would change him. How many women think that? I bet a whole lot of women! How naïve I was. This man was prideful, selfish, and it was his way or the highway. That pretty much sums up not only Chris back then but the majority of men at one time or another. Chris never treated Preston as a son but more like a brother. He played with him and picked on him. This is not what I wanted when I prayed for a provider. I left out the part about a Christian provider and that was the most important thing I should have prayed for finding. I soon would find out I would be doing a lot of praying. I was about to walk through the fire and the flames were hot!

Chapter Ten

Ray of Hope

I got a call one day from the preschool and they told me to come and get my son. The teacher on the phone told me Preston's nose was bleeding, and they could not get it to stop. I went to the preschool, got Preston, and took him to the doctor. He was only four years old at the time. This was in the year of 2000.

I took him to his pediatrician, and he examined Preston. He told me that all boys pick their nose and not to worry. Still, while we were there, he wanted to check out everything. He lifted Preston's shirt, did an abdominal exam, and listened to his heart and lungs. He then looked at me and said, "How long has his stomach been extended with these varices all over it?" "Excuse me, Doctor, but what are varices?" I asked. "The blood vessels that have rerouted their way to get to his heart are varices that have showed up all over his stomach, because it looks as if there might be a blockage of some kind somewhere," the doctor replied.

The doctor said, "I am sending you to Scottish Rite Hospital for a CT scan". My heart just sank to the floor. I took Preston immediately with orders to have the scan done. I called Michael. I called Chris. I probably called my mom, but I don't remember. I was in shock! How could there be anything wrong with my little boy?

I waited as patiently as I could by myself in a hallway for the radiologist to come out and talk with me. He finally came through the door. He said, "Ma'am I'm so sorry, but I think he might have leukemia." I really didn't know what leukemia was at that time. I just knew I wanted to faint. He then said I would need to go to the main hospital for further testing. I got my orders, and we were off again.

This time his dad was with me, and we were expecting the worst. The MRI test came back, and we were told that our little boy would be placed on a liver transplant waiting list for a donation. He had liver failure. He had a diagnosis that I could not pronounce called Primary Sclerosing-Cholangitis. His bile duct connecting to his liver had a tumor on it. That tumor was blocking all blood flow. His liver was shriveling up like an alcoholic's liver, and he was dying. His eyes were yellow. I had no idea. His stomach was enlarged. I thought he was just eating a lot of Happy Meals! I honestly had no idea. What kind of mother would not know something was wrong with her baby?

My son was now placed on a transplant waiting list. Preston looked normal. He played normally. He was dying inside. How scary is that? I started praying. I was angry. I thought God was punishing me for the life I was living. I thought why me God? I cried. I screamed. Where was God?. I cried out to him, and he did not respond.

On April 1, 2000, Michael got a call from the liver team at a children's hospital in Atlanta. The hospital had been trying to reach my cell phone. They told Michael to find me and have me call them immediately. They had found a cadaveric liver for my son, and it was an exact match. Someone's child had died, and they donated their organs for someone else to live. What a gift of mercy! I can't imagine what that family was going through. Michael finally found me after he had been trying to call me to no avail. We literally had a five minute window, or they would have given the liver to someone else. You could see the frantic look on both of our faces. The thought of worry, fear, anxiety, and desperation had now entered our minds.

I remember Preston was in surgery for hours. All of our families were there including our parents, brothers, sisters, cousins, nieces, nephews, and friends. We all were in a circle praying and holding hands. Thank God, He heard our prayer. He saved my son. The doctor came out thirteen hours later and said that Preston would be fine and he was now in intensive care. The doctor allowed Michael and me to go back and see Preston. When I walked in the room, I immediately burst into tears. I thought Michael was going to have to pick me up off the floor. I felt faint. My little boy laid there with tubes coming out of his nose, his neck, his arms, and his side. He was unconscious. He had no idea what had just happened to him. His eyes were closed, and although he was breathing, he looked dead. My God, where are You? As we went into the hallway, I broke down and Michael did, too. We both cried and held each other in the hallway while no one was looking.

Preston was all I had. I did not have a husband. I didn't have a place to call my own. My family lived miles away. Yes, I had a boyfriend, but he was not even my fiancé at the time. I had no one.

I prayed one night, crying out in desperation to God. I told God that if He would save my son that I would start to live for Him the best way that I knew how. Preston was in the hospital for almost two weeks. He had tubes in his nose and neck, and he looked like a limp dish rag. He was going through rejection, but they were pumping him full of medications and strong steroids. His liver enzymes came back on his lab work within somewhat of a normal range and we got to go home. He was almost five years old. He would be starting Kindergarten soon. How do you explain what just happened to a five-year-old easy enough for him to understand?

I remember him asking me if he was going to die. That was hard. How do you even begin? I didn't know Jesus then. I did tell him God was watching over him. I told him that God would heal him. I did what any mother would do. I tried to calm him and ease his fears to the best of my ability. I told him that his liver stopped working so the doctors had to replace it with a new one. We made up a name for it and called it, "Liver Joe". This is what I told Preston. "Every time Liver Joe acts up, we have to go get blood work for the doctors to be able to see what's wrong. That way they can give the right amount of medicine to make Liver Joe feel better and work normally. Your body doesn't want Liver Joe inside of you. Your body wants to kick it out. The medicine you take tells your body that it's okay for Liver Joe to live there." He seemed to understand.

Preston had to have a home health nurse come out and get his blood from his neck port for several weeks. Preston's transplant would require him to stay on medication for the rest of his life. It would require several blood tests every one to six weeks depending on what the liver team at Children's Healthcare of Atlanta would tell us. It was going to require an awful lot on my part of being a mom. I was a single mom. I was a mom without much income who was relying on her boyfriend at the time as a provider. Preston's diagnosis would leave him being immune suppressed. It would mean that he would pick up germs more easily than the average normal child. It would require a lot of hand washing and wearing a mask on occasion if needed. He did not get a chance to complete his four year vaccines; therefore, he was susceptible to Chicken Pox and other viruses.

84

One summer we went to Disney World sponsored by the Make-A-Wish Foundation. We had so much fun. Preston, on the other hand, was very tired and his legs hurt. We had no idea what was in store for us, but knew when we got home he needed to be checked out. He was only six years old at the time and we were told his blood count was low. After about the fourth blood transfusion, I needed answers. I demanded he see another physician who was a hematologist. He specialized in blood disorders. He ran several tests. He had the symptoms of leukemia, but the results came back negative. Instead we found out he contracted the virus Parvo-Human B-Nineteen. It attacked his blood cells. Most people can get the virus and fight it off, but he could not with his immune system so low. They said that the virus was airborne. He breathed it in from someone just coughing or sneezing. Who would have thought that anything like that would happen? It's a lot more than just catching the common cold. He had to get six blood transfusions and two immune gamma globulin infusions to put the virus in remission.

Going to the AFLAC center at the hospital to have his infusions was depressing. We would see cancer children getting their medicine and Preston would look at them and wonder why he was there in the same room. On one visit, they could not find a vein to draw Preston's blood so they started looking at his feet for a vein. He started crying, and I immediately said, "I'm sorry but we will have to come back another day." We left and went home. It was almost a two hour drive. Knowing we would have to go back on another day in the same week didn't bother me. What bothered me was my little boy and the emotional trauma I knew he was enduring.

A few weeks into the blood transfusions, I could tell that Preston was developing emotional anxiety. He had gone through so much. His parents were divorced. He was trying to cope with lab visits, blood draws, and doctors galore. We took him to see a child psychologist recommended by the hospital. He went and expressed his feelings, and the doctor seemed to help him. We did a lot of role playing. We drew pictures. We talked. We listened. We got through it, slowly but surely.

Knock on wood he hasn't had Parvo-Human since, but that was hard to go through. One time he got strep throat. Normally antibiotics will make it go away in three days. With Preston, it took two weeks and a bicillin shot! Looking back at what my son went through, I can truly tell you that God has watched over him. God has a plan for him. Jeremiah 29:11 says: "For I know the plans I have for you says the Lord; plans to give you a hope and a future." To me that verse tells me that I do not know my son's future, but God does. If he didn't have a future, God would have taken him by now.

Since he would be starting Kindergarten in the fall, I wanted him to spend time with his grandmother, Anna, who had a Master's degree in teaching. He went with his dad for the summer, and she taught him how to read. Before he was six years old, he knew how to read on a third grade reading level. She was an amazing woman of wisdom!

Chris and I looked at houses and talked about making a better life for all of us. We found a house in Hill, Georgia. Preston would start school at the elementary school across the street in the fall of 2000. A lot of changes were headed our way. He would soon be in a new house and starting a new school. He had to learn to take medication every day, twelve hours apart. What a heavy weight for me to bear. Why God? I had so many emotions running through me. I felt as if God was repaying me for my horrible past. I was angry. I remember coming home from work one day and crying out to God with tears streaming down my face. I had to pull over off the side of the road because my eyes were flooded with tears and I couldn't see to drive. I turned the radio off and remember clinching my hands tightly on the steering wheel. I was begging Him to take over, to forgive me, to save my son and heal him. My mom was four hours away from me.

Dawn Glaser

My sisters were miles away and so was my dad. I had a boyfriend and coworkers but with very little support at the time. What I needed was Jesus! God was bringing me to my knees and the only thing I could do was look up! I was screaming out loud to God, "What did I do to deserve this?!!!" I sat in silence for a few minutes and heard God speak to me. The answer was evident. He said, "Daughter, I am here." He said that I moved away from Him. He never moved. He was there all the time, waiting for me to call to Him.

I have heard God will not give us more than we can handle. In 1 Corinthians 10:13 Paul tells us that "God is faithful; He will not let you be tested beyond your strength, but with your testing He will also provide a way out so that you may be able to endure it." The weight was heavy, but I knew in my heart God was seeing us through this storm. Every day I would pass by a little country brick church with stained glass windows and would think to myself, "It's very close to home and we need to be there." It reminded me of my grandparent's church that I attended while spending the summers with them. Everyone knew everybody there and welcomed you with a handshake and a smile the moment you walked in. I remember feeling that I needed God in my life more than ever. There was a little country church, "Hope Baptist Church" around the corner from where we lived. Preston and I started to attend. I loved the preacher and his messages. Everyone there was so welcoming and down to earth. Chris would come every now and then but never wanted to become socially involved. Preston attended Awana nights on Wednesdays. He was saved and baptized in that little church, and I rededicated my life to Christ. On the day that Preston was baptized, I noticed that in his hand he had a Bible tract telling how to be saved. He took it and gave it to Chris. I now was starting to look up.

Chapter Eleven

When it Rains, it Pours

I thought that since God had placed Chris in my life, surely I would be able to change him. I thought that I could mold him into the Christian man that I wanted him to be. Can you spell the word "wrong" in big capital letters and put it on a neon flashing sign for me? How many women out there think the same thing? I thought that I would marry him and then he would change. I was now becoming like the woman in the book of Samuel in the Bible named "Abigail". She was loyal without being blind.

We got married on December 22, 2001 in Hill Valley United Methodist Church. We went to the

Biltmore in Asheville, North Carolina for our honeymoon. Things seemed okay at first but then nothing had changed. He was constantly criticizing me and making short comments off the wall toward my son. He always talked about having a nicer car and a nicer and bigger home. He was so prideful and selfish. He felt as if everyone "owed" him. I thought, "When he is ever going to be happy?" I thought that if we got those things, then maybe he would change.

We moved to a bigger home and left our friends behind. Preston had to adjust again and start over in the third grade in a new elementary school. Chris stopped working the night shift which made things better, but he was still the same man that was so lost. He would get mad and fly off the handle at the least little thing. He needed God in his life. I would continually preach to him and nag him about going to church and about Jesus. It just went in one ear and out the other. It seemed like I could never cook the best meal, keep the cleanest house, or do anything right to please him. I was now miserable.

It was going on five years now into our marriage and something had to give. I often wondered why he was like this and where he learned these traits. Was it a generational pattern? I later found out that it was. I remember years ago a lady told me to always look at the man's family before you get married because that will tell you what kind of man you are getting. When was I ever going to learn? I cried. I was depressed. I again became an emotional eater and gained weight. I was still having anxiety attacks. I don't know if they were from fear of my past or fear of the present. Chris said that he believed in God, however, he was far from having a relationship with Jesus. I have known people that were both believers and still went through divorce, had affairs, or had financial difficulties. Is any marriage safe? No. However, if you put God as the head of your household, I believe that you both stand a better chance to stay grounded in your marriage.

In December of 2003, I started praying to God that he would allow me to get pregnant. I felt like Hannah in the book of Samuel in the Bible. She was in turmoil all around her and prayed for a son. I thought if only I could have a child with Chris then it would change his heart toward me and we would become more like a family. Just like Hannah became pregnant, I found out that I was in January 2004. Chris seemed excited about the fact; however, it didn't change his actions. He still had a short fuse, and Preston and I were walking on eggshells around him. The garage door would go up in the evening, we knew that he was home, and we would have a frantic look on our faces. He never hit me; however, the criticism and emotional rollercoaster were enough to just about put me under. He would take off his belt to change clothes as he got home from work. He would look at Preston, and as he was popping the belt, he would smile and say, "Come on Preston, let's go." He would tell Preston that he was just like a puppy dog, and we should put a "for sale" sign on him and stick him in the yard. He would tell me things like, "Look at the dirt on the floor in this kitchen; you call yourself a housewife?"

In the year of 2004, I was at my wits end. I had given up. I still did not have any family here. I was ready to throw in the towel. I asked my father if I could borrow money and he gave it to me. I got a lawyer and drew up the papers. I was ready to call it quits. I had gone to three counselors. One of the counselors told me that I had a bad Ace in my hand. Another counselor told me to go to my local women's shelter for emotional abuse. Another counselor told me it would be a miracle for him to change and I should just start over. My sister Denise told me before I married Chris that I would have a hard row to hoe, and she was right.

Have you ever heard that God is the "ultimate counselor", and he is the one you should turn to in your time of need? I was seeking men and women, friends, or anyone who would listen for guidance. I had one big pot of chicken stew, and every time I got advice from people instead of God, I just added it into my pot of the wrong ingredients. I was not seeking the Lord. All I could do was criticize my husband for the way he treated my son and me. There was no respect for him. My mother was ready to come, pack my stuff, and take me to her house. My family was telling me to leave him. My doctor was telling me to leave him. The counselor was telling me to leave him.

One night Chris came home from work and I arranged for Preston to be with his dad. I gave the divorce papers to Chris, and he said that he would do anything to stay. He cried, and so did I. He knew that I meant business. I told him that I could no longer live with the way he was emotionally mistreating my son or me. I told him I would not allow him to torment us anymore. I told him that I had had enough and was ready to call it quits. I was pregnant with his son at the time. I put everything on the table and told him my stipulations. I wanted him to start treating me like a wife. I wanted him to treat Preston as a friend if he could not treat him as a son. I needed for all of us to attend church. If he could not do those things I would make sure that I had his paycheck and everything he ever worked for in order to raise our unborn child. He immediately agreed to do all of the things I asked. We both cried and prayed that night together. He admitted he was wrong and asked for forgiveness. I tore up the papers and forgave him, but told him that he would have to prove himself to me tremendously. Now he was the one walking on eggshells.

Chris was changing a little but not as quickly as I would have liked. We had a new baby boy named Adam in September 2004. I thought, like most women do, that now that we had a child he would definitely change and be normal. Our marriage was not a marriage. He was barely talking to me. He would come home from work and walk right past me. He would go to bed and not say a word. He would wake up in the morning, leave for work, and never say anything. I probably got to speak five to ten words in a week. One night I got down on my knees and poured my heart out to God in prayer. I turned everything I had in my inner being over to the Lord.

I was now desperate and depressed. One day a girlfriend of mine suggested that I attend a ladies' bible study at our church. I could put my little one in the daycare there while I attended. It was great. They welcomed me and loved on me, and I started to learn more about God and the life I was supposed to live. In one of my classes, I was asked to give my testimony in front of the women. They laid hands on me as I cried in preparation to do so. I stood up and gave a brushed-over testimony of how God restored me, but left out key points that I wanted to carry to my grave. Satan still had a hold on me. A year passed by, and I had joined a ladies' Sunday school class. I felt God tugging at me to make things right, so I volunteered to stand up again and tell my story. This time I told all. I cried, and the release came from me like a waterfall of tears overflowing. In the room listening and crying that day were women from a rehab program. I had women come up to me and tell me how they appreciated my boldness and transparency in telling the truth. The bondage had been broken, and I was no longer captive. I started going to church regularly and grew stronger in my faith.

I was starting to see that I could win my husband over without saying a word like it says in the book of Peter. In 1 Peter 3:1 it states: "Wives, in the same way be submissive to your husbands, so that if any of them do not believe the word, they may be won over without words by the behavior of their wives when they see the purity and reverence of your lives." I remember telling Chris that if he didn't come with us, we were going to leave him behind. He started coming to church. Finally, in 2007 he was saved, baptized, and admitted in front of the whole congregation that he was a sinner and that he was trusting in the Lord to be his personal Lord and Savior. My counselor said that it would take a miracle. My miracle had just come true. Don't ever let anyone tell you that miracles don't happen. I have witnessed quite a few in my life, and this was an answered prayer.

Chris continued to change. He is not perfect, but God was now molding him into the man that I so longed for in my life. God is in control. I am not. God does things in his own timing. God orchestrates everything, and I love to watch his story unfold right before my eyes.

Chapter Twelve

Looking for the Lighthouse

After turning my problems over to God on my knees in prayer, things finally started to look up, and I could see the light in the darkness of the storm. Things were not perfect. Things were better. Chris and I were talking. He found out that he had a diagnosis of attention deficit and needed medication in order to focus on things and think more clearly. Chris was nicer to Preston. He was no longer critical toward me or my son. Chris was changing. I could see little changes in him and was starting to finally fall in love with the man I married. We went on family outings together. We prayed together and took turns praying around the dinner table. We kept going to church and attending church functions. We even taught Sunday School for Adam's class. We were building the kind of marriage we were suppose to have years ago.

Why did it take so long? I believe it was because we were not equally yoked. I did not pray like I should. I did not seek God as the ultimate counselor. I almost gave up. Praise the Lord that he kept us together and now we will be married ten years this December. My mom prayed for her husband's salvation for twenty-three years, and now he is saved. She didn't give up. She hung in there and now they have been married over thirty-three years. I'm glad I am so much like my mom in that respect and hung in there. Otherwise, I would have just kept going around the same mountain and trying to fill the void with the perfect man. Guess what, there's not one!

My grandmother Lynn was married, divorced, and re-married. Her first husband left her. While taking her to work one day, he vanished and never returned. God sent a Christian man to support her and love her. She was a cancer survivor, and she never gave up. She stood like Esther in the Bible and trusted in God to provide, and He did! I always asked her how she got by. Her reply was, "I just suck it up, baby, and kept on going." I think of that often when times get hard, and if she can do it, then I can too!

Prayer is the key. When we pray through Jesus Christ, we have direct access to the throne of God. It is so simple, but people make it so complicated and don't ever think it is powerful enough to redeem them. I was so wrong for thinking that God could not save our marriage. He not only saved our marriage, but He restored it. A weight had been lifted off of my shoulders. I still have to pray often; in fact, I pray daily. Without God, there is no hope. Without hope, there is fear. When you have fear, you can't function.

I'll never forget the time Preston was in the hospital and going through liver rejection. So many people came in to see us, and we honestly thought that he was going to be put back on a waiting list for another liver. They continued to do tests and blood work. One day the phone rang and it was his P.E. teacher from his elementary school. She asked me what I was doing. I told her we were the only ones in the room, and Preston was sleeping. She then asked me to lay my hand on his stomach so she could pray through the phone for Preston. I don't remember exactly what she prayed, but I remember the next morning. The doctor came in and said, "Mrs. Glaser I need to see you in the hallway." I went out expecting the worse. The doctor said that all of his lab results were somehow back to the normal range and he could not explain it. He said he was writing orders for us to go home. I knew then that it came from higher up! I went from sadness to gladness in a matter of seconds! I had just witnessed a miracle. Don't ever think that God Almighty is not in the miracle business anymore. He makes them happen every day. Whether He heals us on earth or decides to heal us by giving us a new body when we get to Heaven; He is Jehovah Rapha, the great physician. I believe in the power of prayer, and so should you.

I make a point to pray out loud so that my children hear me. Sometimes they have witnessed me on my knees praying. My little boy, Adam, told me one morning he couldn't find me but then soon realized that I was in my closet praying. I want my children to know how important it is to seek God with all things as we go through this life. I want them to know when they are uncertain, afraid, or need someone to talk to all they have to do is pray. In the book of Matthew 6: 5-8 it says the following: "When you pray, do not be like the hypocrites, for they love to pray standing in the synagogues, and on the street corners, to be seen by men. However, when you pray go into your room, close the door, and pray to your Father, who is unseen. In addition, when you pray, do not pray like the pagans, for they think they will be heard because of their many words." I want my children to know that God never sleeps and that He is always waiting and always listening. Sometimes He may not give me the answer I am looking for, but I know that something better awaits me.

In Genesis 25:26, it states: "Isaac prayed to the Lord on behalf of his wife, because she was childless. The Lord answered his prayer, and his wife Rebekah became pregnant." Matthew 19:26 states: "Jesus looked at them and said, 'With man all this is impossible, but with God all things are possible.'" God is an awesome God.

Chapter Thirteen

His Anchor Holds

After going to Sunday school and church, and Bible studies for a while, I started to get stronger on the inside. I was sharpening my mind with God's word and didn't even realize I was doing it.

I made many friends at our church. I even got a job there teaching the children in preschool. Things were definitely starting to look up. God was molding me into the woman, wife, and mother he planned for me to be. I always thought it was Chris that needed changing, but it was me. I was wrong. How could I expect someone to change without looking at my own flaws? In the book of Matthew 7:3, it says the following: "Why do you look at the speck of sawdust in your brother's eye, and pay no attention to the plank in your own eye?" I have no right to judge my siblings, my parents, my spouse, or anyone for that matter. I have just as many flaws of my own.

I was in total fear for years. I had anxiety attacks. I listened to psychiatrist after psychiatrist until I was blue in the face. God didn't give up on me. He never let go of me. I love the old hymns talking about how God is always there. He's the lighthouse in the storm. He's the anchor that holds through the storm. He's always there. He's my rock. He is my redeemer. He's my deliverer. That's it! God never let go of me. Through all of the years of highs and lows and the storms that I went through, He was there. He was right there with me the whole time. He never moved. I moved. If only I had reached out my hand, I would have known that His was right beside mine waiting for me to take hold of it. Looking back, I have not forgotten the storms. Thank God, I had enough sense in me to come back to Him. Praise Jesus, I found Him again.

In the fall of 2010, I went to an open house to sign up for a women's Bible study at our church. I thought, "I know I will sign up with the same teacher I am familiar with. She is funny and I like her." As I was walking around and looking for my friends to get them into the same class, a lady pointed something out to me. She said, "It's a shame that so many women don't seek God out to determine what class to join. Instead they treat this like a social event." Ouch! God had spoken to me through His Holy Spirit. He said that I was to get out of the class I signed up for and take another class instead. The class was about defending your minds and marriages. The following Tuesday when I went to sign up for the class, the lady told me it was full and to sign up for something else. I told her that God told me this was the class I should attend. I felt that I would be ready to serve after this one, so I would wait until the following year. By the look on her face, she was dumbfounded. She told me that I could have her seat and that she was not going to argue with God. That's when I met the teacher of my class. She was on fire for the Lord like I had never seen before. She encouraged me. She inspired me to get a backbone for once in my life and take control. She taught me how to defend my mind against Satan and his lies. She was placed in my path by God Almighty, and I am forever grateful, not only for her, but for God placing her in my pathway.

Before the end of October, I was reading a book called "Six Hours One Friday Anchoring to the Power of the Cross" by Max Lucado. I had just finished it while in the waiting room of my psychiatrist. I took it in with me to see him. As I looked around at the books on his shelf, I realized I was seeking the wrong counselor and not the ultimate counselor. There was nothing in his office that was of Christianity. I decided right then and there that my appointment with that doctor would be my very last. I laid my book on his desk as a gift to him and never returned.

In the parking lot as I was leaving the psychiatrist's office, I prayed out loud for God to send me in the right direction to find the deliverance I so desperately needed. As I was listening to the radio on the way home, I heard about a doctor's office in Atlanta that was Christian based and used natural supplements and medicine if needed. I researched their website and read up on the doctors. I also talked with someone from our church that had gone there and was very pleased with her treatment. I liked the profile for one of the doctors named Dr. Tanner and the testimonials of other patients who were treated under her care. She not only believed in homeopathic medicine, but traditional medicine as well. She had an M.D. after her name and I was pleased with her bio and credentials. I made the appointment to go see if they could help me. I signed in and sat down. I could hear Christian music playing in the background. It seemed to be very relaxing and peaceful there. I looked over on the end table and saw a Bible. I knew I was in the right place.

I had made an appointment with Dr. Tanner, but for some reason my appointment got mixed up and I saw another physician that day. He was nice and to the point but talked way too fast for me. I liked what he told me. He told me they were going to help wean me off my meds and find out why my neurotransmitters malfunctioned. He said for me not to worry and have hope. He ordered several lab tests. I had to take a saliva test, blood test, urine, stool sample, and hair sample test to check for thyroid disorders or any underlying conditions I wasn't aware of. I also had a test to check my acid level in my stomach by swallowing a pill they watched go down into my stomach with a special camera and graph test of some kind. I was now ready to make my next appointment with Dr. Tanner.

I chose Dr. Tanner because of her bio and how she had children with illnesses. She was concerned for their well being and wanted to find the underlying cause for their diagnosis. She believed in getting to the root of the problem rather than giving a quick fix with a trial-and-error pill. Most doctors do that these days. If one pill doesn't work, then they find another one until the patient finds relief. She walked in the room with a smile on her face and introduced herself. She had an aura about her that shined. She took the time to answer all of my questions, and she wrote down all of my responses to her questions. She went over all of my lab results. She found that I was lacking vitamins and minerals that helped my brain function. She knew I needed things like zinc, magnesium, vitamin B-12, and selenium. Dr. Tanner got me off all medication and helped me with a diet plan with the right vitamins and minerals that I needed. She went over my results thoroughly and told me what foods I was allergic to and how they could affect me with sleep and headaches. I lost nineteen pounds in six months. I started sleeping better and having more energy.

Dr. Tanner told me to continue to believe in myself, and I would be just fine. She pointed to the necklace I was wearing that had the word " believe" on it. She said that really that's all I had to do. I needed to believe. She was right! All I needed to do was believe in myself! I did not trust in God enough or have the faith of a mustard seed. In the book of Matthew 17:20 it says the following: "He replied, "Because you have so little faith, truly I tell you, if you have faith as small as a mustard seed, you can say to this mountain 'move from here to there, and it will move'. Nothing will be impossible for you." By faith, we can have the indwelling of God's Holy Spirit which will give us power to do the unthinkable for his glory.

Don't get me wrong, I do believe that there are doctors in this world and God gives them the ingenuity to heal certain diseases. I am grateful for my son's doctors and how they are helping him through medication. If he did not have medicine, he would not be here after his liver transplant. However, there are some illnesses that can be cured through the natural elements that God gives us. I feel like we don't have to totally rely on medication. For example, it is proven through research that fish oil is good for your heart, brain, and cholesterol. Instead of taking cholesterol medication I am taking supplements such as krill fish oil. I believe that the measure of my faith in God along with the right doctor is what got my life back on track. I would never want anyone to feel that there is a stumbling block in their life and decide that there is no hope. God is our healer. Psalms 103:3 says the following: "Praise the Lord, my soul; all my inmost being, praise His holy name. Praise the Lord, my soul, and forget not all his benefits, Who forgives all your sins and heals all your diseases, Who redeems your life from the pit and crowns you with love and compassion, Who satisfies your desires with good things so that your youth is renewed like the eagle's."

God will give you hope. In 1 Peter 3:15 it says the following: "But in your hearts, revere Christ as Lord. Always be prepared to give an answer to everyone who asks you to give the reason for the hope that you have. But do this with gentleness and respect." In 1 Peter 1:3 it says the following: "Praise be to God the father of our Lord Jesus Christ! In His great mercy, He has given us new birth into a living hope through the resurrection of Jesus Christ from the dead. That verse tells me that my hope is in Jesus. He died and rose again to give us hope! God will send you the right doctor to give you the help you need! Psalm 37:40 says the following: "The Lord helps them and delivers them; He delivers them from the wicked and saves them, because they take refuge in Him." In John 14:16 it says the following: "And I will ask the father and he will give you another advocate to help you and be with you forever." All you have to do is believe and trust in the Holy Spirit to be your guide! In Luke Chapter 8, the Bible talks about the women who accompany Jesus and His disciples. It says, "the twelve were with Him and also some women who had been cured of evil spirits and diseases: Mary (called Magdalene) from whom seven demons had come out, Joanna the wife of Cuza, the manager of Herod's household; Susanna; and many others." These women were helping to support them out of their own means. I can relate to Mary Magdalene. I think that if she had seven demons come out of her, she must have had spiritual warfare going on in her mind as well. I am grateful to finally be free and thankful that I am able to walk right alongside with Jesus every day!

Dr. Tanner tells me now that she can see a difference in me. She said on my last visit I was glowing. I feel great! God is so good. I still occasionally have symptoms of Bipolar Disorder, but I can control them. For instance, a lot of noise has always bothered me. I cannot stand to be in a room with the television going, hear the kids running and screaming, and the radio blasting at the same time. I am not like some women who can tune out anything annoying. I often need silence. If it bothers me, one of them has to go, or I just remove myself from the situation. Also, I talked with Dr. Tanner about how I am affected by the seasons. In the winter time, I can go into a depressive state if it is cold and dreary outside for several days. She said, it was called, "Seasonal Affective Disorder." She told me to buy some natural sun lamp bulbs, and it would help change the mood around the house. I did, and it works! We don't live near the beach to have sunshine every day, but one day I have hopes of retiring there.

Who would have ever thought that someone who had been raped, lost a child, been divorced, and gone through years of emotional baggage could be medication free? Honestly, it's still hard for me to fathom sometimes. God restored me. God restored my marriage. God healed my son. God watches over me. He is everything to me. Without Him, I would be nothing. I would still be in the pit of depression. What I went through in my life was bittersweet. In the place and time I am in right now, I wouldn't trade anything for what He has blessed me with. I remember once years ago, my psychiatrist said, "miracles are few and far between". That told me right there that he had very little faith. It was a red flag to me that I was not where I was supposed to be and to get out of there as fast as I could. Miracles happen every day, every time a child is born into this world, a flower blooms, a bee makes honey, and the list goes on.

God is our creator. He makes miracles happen. I have faith in Him and feel sorry for people who don't. God made me. God saved me! God redeemed my life and gave me purpose. That's a miracle that I am grateful for each and every day. In the book of Job 9:10 it states: "He performs wonders that cannot be fathomed, miracles that cannot be counted." He changed my whole being and character. He transformed my mind and renewed it. Romans 12:2 says: "Do not conform to the patterns of this world, but be transformed by the renewing of your mind. Then you will be able to test and approve what God's will is, His good, pleasing and perfect will."

The Bible teaches us that Jesus came to heal our wounds, broken hearts, give us joy, and turn our ashes into beauty. (See Isaiah 61:1-3.) This kind of beauty will never fade within us, and it can only come through Jesus. Only God could have taken the ashes I chose to create of myself and make me whole and beautiful again.

He gave me the characteristics of Him. That's the fruit of the spirit that you can only receive once you ask Jesus into your life. Galatians 5:22 says: "But the fruit of the spirit is love, joy, peace, forbearance, kindness, goodness, faithfulness, gentleness, and self control." Second Corinthians 5:5 says: "Now the one who has fashioned us for this very purpose is God, who has given us the spirit as a deposit, guaranteeing what is to come." I was even like the Samaritan woman at the well who had many husbands and didn't seek his face first. Once I started placing the Lord of my life, I didn't need to go to the well for water anymore. Jesus was all the water I ever needed and I am now only thirsty for him!

If He loved me enough to save someone like me, He can save you too. He's waiting. All you have to do is ask. Won't you allow Him to turn your life around? Are you tired of trying to fill the void with those of the opposite sex, alcohol, food, drugs, money, smoking and the like? He will give you living water overflowing. It's time to set down your water jar at the feet of Jesus. He's waiting for you just like He was for me. I can relate to so many of those women with my past, but now I am a new person. I sometimes see myself like Lydia, who opens her home to perfect strangers. My grandmother was known for this. I see myself like Martha who is much like my mother. She is always busy, yet treats others with hospitality. As she grows older, she learns to listen and that silence is golden. I also see myself like my grandmother, Lynn. She was much like Esther who had the courage to stand. She lost her first born son shortly after birth. She went through her first marriage married to a man whom she loved dearly and who left her without a trace after raising my mother and years of marriage. God sent her another man who was a Christian for over forty years before she was called to go home to Heaven. She was a breast cancer survivor. She was truly an inspiration! The raindrops in my life may have been bittersweet, but now the security from the lighthouse promises me hope that could only have come from God. In the Bible, Hebrews 6:19 says the following: "We have this hope as an anchor for the soul, firm and secure. God is our anchor through this storm called "life", and the anchor holds!" In the book of Psalms 107:29 it says the following: "He stilled the storm to a whisper; the waves of the sea were hushed." He stilled the storm within me, and I promise he can do the same for you. All you have to do is believe!

Chapter Fourteen

How to Become a Christian

God loves you so much that he sent his only son Jesus to die for your sins. Romans 5:8 says the following: "God demonstrates His own love for us in this: while we were yet sinners, Christ died for us." Titus 3:5 says the following: "He saved us not because of righteous things we had done, but because of his mercy." God allows us to come to Him through His grace. He offers a gift through his son Jesus. We can't save ourselves by trying to be a better person. Only God can rescue us!

Ephesians 2:8-9 says the following: "For it is by grace you have been saved, through faith; and not from yourselves; it is the gift from God, not by works so that no one can boast." Jesus paid your penalty by dying on the cross for you. He paid your sin debt. In Romans 6:23 it says the following: "For the wages of sin is death, but the gift of God is eternal life through Jesus Christ our Lord." God raised Jesus from the dead after He died on the cross.

All you have to do is confess you are a sinner, believe in Him, and repent. Repent means to change. Change your way of thinking and turn from the sins you know are wrong. When you ask

Jesus to come into your heart and forgive you, He will deposit his Holy Spirit inside of you to help you do this. Ephesians 1:13-14 says this: "And you were included in Christ when you heard the word of the truth, the gospel of your salvation. Having believed, you were marked in Him with a seal, the promised Holy Spirit, who is a deposit guaranteeing our inheritance until the redemption of those who are God's possession; to the praises of His glory."

Romans 10:9-10 says this: "If you confess with your mouth, Jesus is Lord, and believes that God raised him from the dead, you will be saved. For it is with your heart you believe, and are justified, and it is with your mouth that you confess and are saved." John 3:16 says this: "For God so loved the world that He gave his only begotten son, that whosoever believes in Him, should not perish but have everlasting life."

Won't you ask him into your heart today and secure your eternal future? Won't you be sure that when you die your soul is going to Heaven and not Hell? All you have to do is say a simple prayer such as this one below:

Lord Jesus, I know I'm a sinner and don't deserve eternal life. I know that You died on the cross, shed your blood for my sins, and rose again to save me and prepare a place for me to live with You forever. Take control of my life, come into my life, and forgive me of my sins. Make me a new person and help transform my mind into a new way of thinking and living for You. I am trusting in You as my Savior for my salvation and accept Your free eternal gift. In Your name I pray, Amen.

If you just prayed this prayer, please tell someone. Find a local Bible-believing church and attend. Pray to God daily and read His Bible, which is his love letter to you, and you will hear Him speak to you through His word and Holy Spirit. In addition, our role is to witness to others about the love of Jesus. Tell the good news! This is your purpose in life here on earth. This is God's plan.

If you prayed that simple prayer, then I want to welcome you to the family of God! You are now my brother or sister in Christ. May God continue to pour out His love to you!

Blessings!

He Stilled the Storm Within Me

Here are seven devotions from my upcoming book, "Daybreak Devotions" to be released sometime in 2012.

Day One

Kept Alive

While watering my flowers yesterday, I looked over at the plant that my grandmother gave me before she died. I was amazed at the thought of how it had been kept alive. You see, when my grandmother got married in the 1930's her mother gave her this plant as a wedding gift. For the fifty-two years that she was married to my grandfather, she nurtured it and kept it alive. She watered it, she gave it the tender loving care that it needed, and plant food weekly in order for it to survive. After my grandfather passed away she continued to nourish the plant another twenty-two years before she was called home to Heaven. Two weeks prior to her passing, I went to visit her and she wanted to give me the plant. I said, "Nanny, I don't have a green thumb. Are you sure you want me to have it?" She said, "Just water it twice a week and you will be fine." Well, guess what? So far so good. I am amazed that I have not let her down. When thinking of the plant I also was thinking about our mind, body, and how we are kept alive in relation to the plant. You see, it made me think that once you've

113

accepted Christ as your savior you have to take care of your body with the proper nourishment that it needs because your body is the temple where Jesus resides. Also, you have to water your mind daily with his living water and saturate it with his word. In doing so, you will keep the enemy at bay and stamp God's word on your heart and in your mind so that you can retain it. When you go into battle with a crisis just like the plant in the boiling sun in the heat of the day, the water protects it just as God's living water protects you. The word of God speaks of water seven hundred and twenty-two times throughout the bible. It speaks of purification of the Christian. It speaks of water as spiritual life to the Christian. In the book of Genesis 1:2 it first mentions water and how God hovered over it. In Ephesians 5:6 it talks about how we might be cleansed by the washing of the water of the word. In John 4:14 it talks about how you will never thirst if you stay in his word. In revelation it says how if you come to him to take the water of life freely. Do you want to be kept alive? Do you want to never have to go thirsty in the noon day sun? Then simply, get in God's word daily and let it saturate your very soul.

Day Two

Being Afraid

Some people are in fear of a lot more than others. It could be anything from heights, to darkness, to even small spiders. I recently started thinking about other people's fears and not so much focusing on mine. My youngest son has to have his nightlight on for fear of the dark. I have to admit things look a whole lot better in the light, that's for sure! I have never really noticed my oldest son scared of anything much until recently. He is 16 years old. He is really muscular from lifting weights and he pretty much brags about being stronger than me (with a smile of course). Well, this past week I was downstairs. He came running downstairs with his cousin, who is 16 as well, and they both were screaming for me. I thought 'what in the world is going on'. Turns out I had to kill a hornet that had came into his room through the cracked window. Now I know my son has a whole lot of strength but when it comes to bees, spiders, and snakes he turns into a little boy again in an instant. I have never laughed so hard at the two of them this past week. Also, my husband went out in the kayak and a black snake swam underneath his boat. He immediately held his legs way up in the air and was frightened. Fear. Where does it come from? To the woman who has a fear of being attacked and is tormented with it for years it's a pretty scary thing. To the man who is in fear of losing his job. To the woman who just lost her husband and doesn't know how she's going to

Dawn Glaser

make ends meet. To the family whose home was just foreclosed on. To the child who was just diagnosed with a life threatening illness. Fear. I have heard that the word "fear" is mentioned in the bible 366 times. That is a bible verse every day including leap year so that you cannot forget that God says to Fear not! My sister told me several years ago about the verse 2 Timothy 1:7. It says, "For God did not give us a spirit of fear, but of power, of love, and of a sound mind." Did you hear that? If He didn't give it to us, then where in the world is it coming from? Satan! He puts fear in our minds of the unknown when we don't trust in Almighty God. We see it on television through the media and it becomes part of our children's minds. We hear it in listening to the wrong music. I can find enough depression in one country song to last a whole year! My greatest fear, I think, would be to lose my family. I would go through all of the emotions of fear, anxiety, anger, depression, uncertainty, and sadness. However, in the end God would pick me up, stand me back on my feet, and encourage me to be a light to those who are going through the same thing. I am trusting in my Savior. Are you?

Day Three

Leaving a Legacy

I recently visited my mom in South Georgia. One morning I had to go down to Bob's Country Store. When I did, the cashier asked who I was. When I told her whose daughter I was, she immediately told me great things about my mother. She told me how well respected she was in the community. She told me that my mother would do anything for anybody and would go out of her way in the process. She introduced me to everyone in the store as Carroll's daughter. The same day while at my mom's antique shop I met the owner next door. When he realized whose daughter I was, he immediately told me I had "fine" parents. I felt honored. I felt privileged. Tonight while at a dinner, the hostess had her mom attending. She also had her children serving. At the end of the dinner her mother said wonderful things of her daughter. I couldn't help but notice how beautiful she was. I noticed not only was she proud of her daughter, but of her grandchildren as well. Look at the legacy she is passing down. What are you doing for your children? Are you leaving a legacy for them to follow that will glorify God? Did you know that we are daughters of the King? In Ephesians 1:5 it says: "He predestined us to be adopted as his sons through Jesus Christ, in accordance with his pleasure and will." In Galatians 3:28-29 it says: "There is neither Jew nor Greek, slave nor free, male nor female, for you are all one in Christ Jesus. If you belong to Christ, then you are Abraham's seed, and heirs according to the promise." In Romans 8:17 it says: "Now if we are children, then we are heirs—heirs of God and co-heirs with Christ, if indeed we share in his sufferings in order that we may also share in his glory." In 1 Peter 2:9 it says: "You are a chosen people, a royal priesthood, a holy nation, a people belonging to God, that you may declare the praises of him who called you out of darkness into his wonderful light." We are set apart. We are a chosen people. We were purchased for a purpose and were consecrated by God for his possession. There is a song by Nicole Nordeman called "Legacy". Some of the lyrics are as follows: "I want to leave a legacy. How will they remember me? Did I choose to love? Did I point to you enough to make a mark on things?" God has already left us an inheritance through his son, Jesus. Once you become a believer, you are adopted in to the family of God. It gives me great joy to know I am a daughter of the King. I want my children to see Him in me as well as others. I want to leave a legacy. Don't you?

Day Four

Roots

While driving to town today I noticed a tree that was on the edge of a bank. You could see its roots below ground level for at least fifteen to twenty feet. I thought 'man those roots really run deep.' Isn't that how it is with the roots of bitterness? Have you ever been bitter toward someone and you just can't seem to shake it? With friends it's pretty easy to just stop being friends and find new ones. However, with family you can't do that as easily. Have you ever held a grudge toward someone? Can't seem to forgive them? In Hebrews 12:15 it says: "See to it that no one falls short of the grace of God and that no bitter root grows up to cause trouble and defile many." If you just stopped talking to that person it would not be enough, because the bitterness is still there. Just like the root. If you simply cut it in half it is still there and can grow back. You have to dig the entire root up to prevent it from growing back. Unless you completely forgive another person that has wronged, you the bitterness will never go away. God says we must forgive. In Matthew 6:15 it says: "But if you do not forgive others their sins, your Father will not forgive your sins." It's easy to make mistakes. In Romans 3:23 it says: "for all have sinned and fall short of the glory of God." Even though we fall short, God forgives us through his grace. Ephesians 1:7 says: "In him we have redemption through his blood, the forgiveness of sins, in accordance with the riches of God's grace." Acts 13:38 says: "Therefore, my friends, I want you to know that through Jesus the forgiveness of sins is proclaimed to you." If we are to be like Christ, don't you think it's time to get out your gardening tools and dig those roots up? Pray for God to forgive you for being bitter. Pray for God to soften your heart towards that person. Pray for God to help you get past the past and look toward the future. If it's someone who can't forgive you and has pretty much written you out of their life then all you can do is ask for forgiveness, pray, and leave it God's hands. My knees have been dirty from digging up roots, but now I can wear my Sunday best with a smile. Praise the Lord!

Day Five

When it Rains it Pours

My mom always has told me for years, "Don't get out your umbrella until it starts to rain". What she means is not to worry more than you have to. I had a friend tell me once if Noah had waited on the rain to pull out his umbrella he would have been in a mess. Great point. It's all about being prepared. God sends the rain when we need it. It's up to us to receive it and weather the storm to the best of our ability. There are a lot of trials in this life. I have gone through many. I have lost loved ones, been through divorce, lost jobs, just to name a few. The one that is the hardest for me is taking care of my son who has a life threatening illness. It's a constant up and down journey. Sometimes it just mists rain. Sometimes it storms. Sometimes it hails. Sometimes we get to see the rainbow. My son had to have a liver transplant at age four. He is now sixteen. He is doing well for the moment. He has been through blood transfusions, rejection, and several viruses. He also has played baseball, tee ball in elementary school and junior varsity in high school. Looking on the outside you would never know anything was wrong. Sometimes though on the inside the doctors tell us things aren't what they should be. He takes medications. He has blood work often. We do what the doctors say and ride out the storm. I used to worry and fret. It took several years not to do that. Now, I just praise God for every day he's given me with my son and we just keep pressing on. In

Leviticus 26:4 it says: "I will send you rain in its season, and the ground will yield its crops and the trees their fruit." Without the rain there would be no harvest. Without the rain there would be no joy. We have to have the rain in our lives so that we can praise God for the sunshine when the storm is over. Matthew 7:25 says: The rain came down, the streams rose, and the winds blew and beat against that house; yet it did not fall, because it had its foundation on the rock. Although it continues to rain on us through trials and tribulations while we are here on this earth, God is our shelter in the storm. If you have Jesus as your foundation you can weather any storm that may come your way. He is the cornerstone. All you have to do is be prepared for the storm that's going to come at some point in your life when you least expect it. Put on your shield, hold on to your faith, and trust in the Lord to see you through it.

Day Six

What's in a Name

Over our summer vacation we were in Florida and while traveling on our way back home we almost had an accident, along with several other cars. We were the ones who caused it. We had a roof rack on our car with a kayak tied down to it. In an instant the wind carried it off and behind us cars swerved off the road to try and avoid it. No one was hurt, but it was a very scary dilemma. One lady hit our boat and had a flat tire. We got off the next exit and immediately turned around to go help and see what we could do. A department of transportation worker stopped to help us. Guess what his name was? His name was Jeremiah. I knew after he told me his name we were all going to be just fine. We ended up giving our boat to Jeremiah and money to the lady with the flat tire. We were bummed about the boat with no way to get it back home but thankful no one was injured. I talked with Jeremiah briefly and asked him had he ever read the bible verse Jeremiah 29:11. He said no but said that he would look it up on his cell phone after we left. In the bible God tells us that Jeremiah was called to be a prophet. He was set apart. In Jeremiah 1:5 it says: "Before I formed you in the womb I knew you, before you were born I set you apart; I appointed you a prophet to the nations." Jeremiah was strong, courageous, faithful and obedient to the Lord. I wonder when his mother had him did she know of the book in the bible about Jeremiah. When I told

123

my mom of the accident she asked me if we were all ok. I said, "yes God sent Jeremiah to help us." My first son's middle name is David. It is a family name passed down from his father's middle name. I feel sure it was chosen from the bible in reference to King David. David had a heart for God. He was a king who led God's people by God's principles, and God blessed him greatly. I can only hope one day that my Preston David will have a heart for God in the same manner. My other son is named Adam. His name came straight from the bible as you must know in Genesis. His name is special because it was the first name chosen by God. Also, in the book of 1 Corinthians 15:45 it says: So it is written: "The first man Adam became a living being"; the last Adam, a life-giving spirit. The second Adam is referring to Jesus. I pray our little Adam will grow up to be the Christian man, father, and husband that God has called him to be. The next time you are introduced to someone and they tell you their name, dig a little deeper. There just might be some meaning on that name to give you some insight worth investigating.

Day Seven

Blind but Able

Have you ever known anyone who was blind? Years ago I met a lady named Pat who was. She was born blind. She never knew what it was like to see colors and God's creations. She amazed me because at that time she seemed to be in her fifties. She lived alone in an apartment in Atlanta. She had a seeing eye dog that assisted her. She was a strong woman to me. It seems if you lose one of your other senses then you rely on the remainder of them. Your hearing becomes very sensitive. My heart goes out to people who are blind. I used to work for an ophthalmologist years ago, and we had some patients who had very little sight due to glaucoma or macular degeneration. It is sad to know that once you've seen God's creations and lose your sight you will never be able to experience them again. In the book of Luke 7:21 it says the following: "At that very time Jesus cured many who had diseases, sicknesses and evil spirits, and gave sight to many who were blind." In the book of Matthew 15:30 it says the following: "Great crowds came to him, bringing the lame, the blind, the crippled, the mute and many others, and laid them at his feet; and he healed them." Can you imagine the excitement once they could see for the first time In their life? I would be shouting it from the roof tops, "I'm healed"! In Matthew 20:30 it says the following: "Two blind men were sitting by the roadside, and when they heard that Jesus was going by, they shouted, 'Lord, Son of David, have mercy on us!'" They used their sense of hearing and when they knew he was near they knew he would heal them. It took me thirty three years in my life to realize that Jesus would heal me. I wasn't blind, but I couldn't see so to speak. Until I came to know who Christ really was and grasp the concept of the cross I might as well have been blind. In the book of Acts 9:17-19 it says: "Then Ananias went to the house and entered it. Placing his hands on Saul, he said, 'Brother Saul, the Lord—Jesus, who appeared to you on the road as you were coming here—has sent me so that you may see again and be filled with the Holy Spirit.' Immediately, something like scales fell from Saul's eyes, and he could see again." He got up and was baptized, and after taking some food, he regained his strength. Just like Saul was healed you can be healed as well. You can be out of bondage from your past and see Jesus. All you have to do is believe and call on him. You may not see him, but he sees you. In Acts 3:16 it says the following: "By faith in the name of Jesus, this man whom you see and know was made strong." It is Jesus' name and the faith that comes through him that has completely healed him, as you can all see. Won't you open up your eyes and call out to him? He's closer than you think.

CPSIA information can be obtained at www.ICGtesting.com
Printed in the USA
LVOW031638261211

261020LV00001B/3/P